KINGS OF WARWICK

Best wishes

Jean Field

2ʳᵈ May 1995.

*THE UNFORGETTABLE FACE OF KING HENRY VIII WHO RULED FROM 1509
to 1547 AND HAD SIX WIVES, TWO OF WHOM WERE BEHEADED ON HIS
ORDERS. This excellent portrait after Holbein, which hangs in the Court House, was given
to the town by John Bohun Smyth, Mayor of Warwick from 1811 to 1819. (Photograph by
Simon Photography, Warwick)*

KINGS OF WARWICK

by

JEAN FIELD

AN ILLUSTRATED HISTORY TO MARK THE 450th ANNIVERSARY
OF THE CHARITY OF KING HENRY VIII AND WARWICK'S
FIRST CHARTER

BREWIN BOOKS

First published in 1995 by Brewin Books, Studley, Warwickshire.

THE FRONT COVER SHOWS KING HENRY VIII AND AN ENGRAVING
OF WARWICK CASTLE AND THE GREAT BRIDGE IN 1729
BY S. AND N. BUCK.
(This engraving is reproduced by permission of Birmingham City Archives)

ISBN 1 85858 051 X Hardback
ISBN 1 85858 052 8 Paperback

The publication of this book has been facilitated by a grant from the
Trustees of King Henry VIII's Charity in Warwick in recognition of the
450th anniversary of the Charity.

CONTENTS

This book is dedicated to my mother, many of whose ancestors
lived in or near the town of Warwick in centuries past.

The Trustees of Warwick Municipal Charities have been pleased to support the publication of this book, which is intended to mark the 450th Anniversary of the grant of the Letters Patent by King Henry VIII which led to the formation of this Charity. This work, now produced by Jean Field, suggests that the content may have a wider appeal than was first thought, and it is hoped that it will be enjoyed by students of local and national history as well as those who have their roots and interests in Warwick and Warwickshire.

The Trustees wish to state that the opinions expressed in this book are those of the author and do not necessarily represent the views of the Trustees either as a body or individually. Likewise, the facts stated in the book are believed to be correct and based on such information as is available and researched, but no responsibility can be accepted by the Trustees for any errors or ommissions.

Peter Butler
Clerk & Receiver   December 1994

THE FORMER GUILDHALL IN THE LORD LEYCESTER HOSPITAL AS PHOTOGRAPHED BY THE AUTHOR IN 1992. *This building is important to the history of Warwick for it was probably in this hall that the Guild of Warwick held numerous discussions prior to the granting of the first Charter to the town on 15th May 1545. From 1545 until 1571 when the entire group of buildings including Westgate Chapel was granted to the Earl of Leycester for use as a hospital for elderly soldiers, the Corporation of Warwick held their meetings there. Within the past few decades some former guild rooms have once again been used for public functions and on a few important occasions the Town Council has met in the building.*

In 1993 when the building was re-roofed using new materials, the perennial dilemma of conservationists was illustrated. As with numerous other listed buildings in the town, King Henry VIII's Charity made a grant towards restoration work.

INTRODUCTION

15TH MAY 1545 WAS A VERY SPECIAL DAY FOR THE TOWN OF WARWICK. On that day Letters Patent and a Charter signed by King Henry VIII established what is now known as The Charity of King Henry VIII and the Town Corporation, men of the inner body of which were to administer the Estates given by the king for the benefit of the town.

A Brief History

King Henry VIII was in the process of abolishing wealthy religious establishments and confiscating their estates, turning them into revenue for himself. In 1544 the Collegiate Church of St Mary in Warwick voluntarily gave up its extensive estates not waiting for the king to make confiscation orders. Also the United Guild of Warwick sold some land so that a town Charter could be purchased from the king.

The Guild Master, charismatic Thomas Oken negotiated for a settlement, with the result that on 15th May 1545, the Letters Patent set up the Charity bearing the king's name and endowing it with much of the property previously owned by St Mary's Church. The town Charter set up the Corporation, then known as "The Burgesses of Warwick" who were to act as Trustees of the Charity, for the benefit of the town. A month later, the Guild of Warwick (also under threat of abolition by the Crown) transferred its property to the Charity, thereby saving those estates for the town.

The Estate of King Henry VIII and the Guild

Since King Henry VIII only restored to the town what was rightfully belonging in the first place, historians have suggested that a more proper name instead of King Henry VIII's Charity would be "The Estate of King Henry VIII and the Guild". However as alternative names are confusing, I shall refer to the organisation by its usual name today, that is "The Charity of King Henry VIII".

By the Charter of 1554, the Bailiff was granted other revenues from market tolls and rents from the Booth Hall. This Bailiff's fund was supposed to be kept separate from the main Charity, as was money from Thomas Oken's own charity after he had died in 1573. By leaving money for some Civic purposes, it was obvious that Oken intended some of his Charity money to supplement the general Corporation fund.

However as the same inner circle of 12 men were controlling the various funds, it soon became impossible to differentiate between the sources of income. As long as the money was available, the Burgesses were not too fussy which fund it was actually derived from, and in times of hardship or extra expense there was a great deal of transfer and borrowing.

From 1545 to 1835, King Henry VIII's Charity supplied the bulk of the money for Corporation expenditure which included paying the stipends of the clergy, administering the grammar school, entertaining Royalty and providing street lighting.

As there were no regular auditors in the early days, the Corporation members did exactly as they saw fit… which almost always depended on the wishes of the Earls of Warwick. Over the centuries the Earls kept tight control of the town, as they had done in feudal times. To complicate matters further, the Chief Burgesses were in charge of all the town's other major charities besides the Charity of King Henry VIII and Oken's Charity.

As I believe it is the only way to portray a true picture, I have taken the broadest view of the history of the town in order to illustrate how things happened and were funded. Ironically, whenever powerful men were annoyed with the Corporation or the Rulers of the Castle, a complaint was made to Chancery and several times the Corporation was censured for mismanagement of the finances. Indeed in 1737, control of King Henry VIII's Estate was taken from the Corporation for around 25 years. I have no doubt that from time to time, as with large organisations today, corrupt and dishonest men committed fraudulent practices and money was unwisely spent on lavish banquets. However these problems still occur widely today and on the whole it seemed that, even if some members were apathetic or lazy, the Corporations managed as well as could have been expected over the centuries.

Apart from being the largest landowner, which meant that they could exert great power over their tenants, one of the ways in which many of the Earls managed to control the town was by being nominated as Recorder… in charge of law and order in the borough. The post was a nominal one and did have a small salary, but in effect the Deputy Recorder or Town Clerk who was chosen by the Recorder was the powerful man who carried out many of the official duties. The Mayor too was usually a Tory who was acceptable to the Earl who thus wielded enormous power over the Corporation and thereby the town finances, including King Henry VIII's Charity.

1835 onwards.

From 1835 there was a gradual decline in the range and importance of the Charity of King Henry VIII. Following the Municipal Corporations Act, the Charity was placed in the hands of Trustees, who were separate from the Council and more and more money was found for the town finances from other sources, such as local taxes. In the later 19th century many properties were sold by the Charity and from 1875 much money was transferred to the King's Schools Scheme. For much of the twentieth century the charity profits were relatively small, often insufficient to cover traditional expenditure, but in the 1980s land was sold for a huge profit. For the past six years distributable income of over one million pounds annually has been shared by St Mary 's Church (together with the other Church of England churches in the Borough and also Budbrooke) the Warwick Schools Foundation and the town generally.

Why Celebrate the 450th Anniversary?

Centenaries are the obvious celebration times, but older readers will instantly remember why the 400th Anniversary was not a lavish affair. 15th May 1945 was only 7 days after V.E. Day when the much longed-for peace in Europe took effect after nearly 6 bitter years of fighting in the Second World War and most people in Warwick had their minds on other matters. Cessation of hostilities with Japan was still over 3 months away, money was still very tight and food and many other commodities were still rationed.

However 15th May 1995 seems a particularly sensible time for celebrations and a 450th anniversary must be more worthy than a 400th. Sometimes in today's modern world, history is forgotten and the deeds of those to whom we owe so much go unheralded. In this book I hope to redress the balance as far as Warwick is concerned and by giving a selection of the historical details, show the world just what an important date we are celebrating.

A Huge Subject

Although this volume is primarily concerned with the Charity of King Henry VIII, it is impossible to separate this subject from the general history of the town itself. With the Mayor and Corporation acting as the Trustees of the Charity and the income providing the bulk of the money for running the town until 1835, almost every major building in the town has at some time or another been directly connected with the charity. So there are numerous places to describe and wonderful tales to tell.

I could easily fill ten volumes with the many details which I have discovered from my research, but of necessity these facts must be limited to fit the size of the book. Therefore this work will be merely a short guide to enable readers to realise the great scale of the Charity and those fired with enthusiasm can discover further details for themselves.

Miss E. Tibbits

A member of the Tibbits family to whom I owe a great debt is octogenarian Miss Elizabeth Tibbits, a cousin of the late E.G. Tibbits to whom I shall make frequent reference.

Coming from a family which has completed two centuries of continuous public service to Warwick, Miss Tibbits spoke of the vast amount of local history which she had learned from her grandfather John Tibbits and her father Hubert Tibbits. Both had been doctors in Warwick, as was her brother the late Stephen Tibbits who was the local Coroner for many years. During my recent talks with Elizabeth Tibbits,

Warwick history became clearer as I began to understand many of the finer points of the Warwick Corporation, the charities and in particular the personalities about whom I was writing.

It is a historian's dream to be given first hand accounts of many important happenings and to hear Miss Tibbits describe how as a child she had sat on Frances Countess of Warwick's knee, or how her father had attended Warwick School when its premises were in the old College in the Butts, was indeed an inspiration. Amongst other family members who had served on the Corporation and Town Council, her grandfather, uncle, cousin and brother had been Trustees of King Henry VIII's Charity. She herself is still a Trustee of some other important Warwick Charities. As the other members of the Tibbits family now live elsewhere, Elizabeth remains the sole representative in Warwick and I reflected how fitting it was that she should supply many of the details about events which had been the immediate concern of her ancestors.

Kings and Queens of Warwick

I love Warwick and I hope this book will enable others to look on the town with greater interest. As the subject matter is so complex, it is quite conceivable that despite my best efforts, errors have crept into this text. Whilst every effort has been made to ensure these have been eliminated, readers will understand that trying to organise a book of this type is no easy matter.

For several centuries my ancestors have lived in or around the town of Warwick and I am proud to say that I was educated at the King's High School For Girls. Although I travelled the world in my younger days whilst a crew member of various ships, I chose to return to teach in Warwick for many years and being asked by the Trustees to write this book, I feel very privileged. In these pages I have tried to include albeit a brief reference to most of the important facts, but I have also tried to do justice to those worthies who might familiarly be termed KINGS (AND QUEENS) OF WARWICK ... those who did so much for the town and the Charity of King Henry VIII.

GENERAL HISTORY 1545-1835

"We give thanks today for the steadfastness, integrity and generosity of Thomas Oken to whom we are all debtors."

So said the priest in one of the responses at the special service in St Mary's Church on 30th July 1973 to mark the 400th anniversary of Thomas Oken's death and also the 850th anniversary of St Mary's Church, where Oken worshipped and was buried.

We do not know very much about the life of Thomas Oken, except that he was born of humble parents in Warwick, but eventually he became a very wealthy mercer, trading in malt and cloth. He was a respected member of the Warwick Guild and in 1544 he became the Guild Master, entrusted with undertaking difficult negotiations with the King's agents. He presided over the change over from Guild to Corporation and was the very first Principal Burgess in Warwick.

The Year 1545

1545 was the year when the 'Mary Rose' sank. England was at war with France and Scotland and King Henry VIII had been on the throne for 36 years. After being (re?)discovered by Christopher Columbus just over 50 years previously, the American continent was becoming increasingly important, but as yet no one in England knew of the existence of Australia or New Zealand. For many people in England, life was a struggle and early death from malnutrition, harsh punishment, plague or smallpox was common.

King Henry himself had changed from a handsome and talented youth of 18 as he had been when he first came to the throne in 1509 to a fat tyrant, so uncertain of temper that he had had two of his six wives beheaded. In 1543 the ailing king had married Catherine Parr who seemed more of a nurse than a wife and having been extremely extravagant throughout his life, Henry was in serious financial trouble.

The country was still reeling from previous laws passed at the king's insistence. In 1533 he had divorced the Roman Catholic Queen Catherine of Aragon and married Protestant Ann Boleyn. The Pope had excommunicated Henry, but in November 1534 he had conferred on himself the title of Supreme Head of the Church of England. Both extreme Catholics and extreme Protestants were persecuted by Henry who would tolerate no one who would not agree to his new laws. Obviously most people in the land were Catholics as they always had been, but his subjects soon learned to obey the king. Needing more money, the king then passed laws confiscating lands held by religious establishments and it was rumoured that the powerful Guilds were to be abolished and their possessions seized. It was in this climate of change and uncertainty that Thomas Oken began negotiations on behalf of Warwick. Being a merchant connected with the cloth trade, he would have travelled extensively and he probably gained greater knowledge of proposed future legislation as a result.

Warwick in 1545

Warwick at that time was a town of around 2,500 inhabitants, with only two parishes … St Mary's and St Nicholas'. Warwick, as now, had two gates, Eastgate and Westgate, with the Northgate (which is believed to have been between the site of Northgate House and the Police Station) already having been demolished. The Great Bridge (the ruins of which still remain) stood instead of a South Gate and parts of the town wall still remained round the gates. The medieval ditch which had surrounded the walls was not yet completely filled in and The Butts area was being used for organised archery practice. The Beauchamp Chapel was then less than 100 years old, having been begun in 1442 and there were still many houses in the town with thatched roofs and also numerous barns.

The First Charter is Signed on 15th May 1545

For around a year prior to the Letters Patent and the Charter being signed by King Henry VIII, delicate negotiations were carried out. Some 18 months before the passing of the Chantries Act which would have confiscated its property anyway, St Mary's Collegiate Church voluntarily gave up all possessions, some time between April and July 1544 according to E.G. Tibbits. Thomas Oken became Master of the Guild at Michaelmas (29th September) 1544 … presumably he was selected as the best person to secure a good deal for Warwick. As the Head of the Common Council of the Guild of Warwick Thomas Oken must have organised the selling of some Guild land in order to buy the Charter from the king. Apart from this, the new Corporation when formed had to agree to pay £6 13sh 4d to the crown annually.

Thus the town of Warwick was given a Charter which outlined its government by the Burgesses of the town who elected one of their number to be the Principal Burgess. The new Corporation had as finance the lands and privileges granted to the town in "The Charity of King Henry VIII". By no means all the lands given up by St Mary's Collegiate Church were granted back to the town, but many of them were.

King Henry The Eighth's Charity
(quoted from "The Charities of Warwick" … 1826)

"By Letters Patent of King Henry the Eighth, bearing the date the 15th May, in the 37th year of his reign, whereby the inhabitants of the town of Warwick were

incorporated by the name of "The Burgesses of the town of Warwick, in the County of Warwick," the said king granted to the said Burgesses the Rectory and Church of St Mary, and the Rectory and Church of St Nicholas with their rights, members, and appurtenances, within the said town of Warwick, in the county of Warwick, to the late college of St Mary in the same town of Warwick, then dissolved and surrendered, lately belonging and appertaining, and lately being parcel of the possessions or revenues thereof; and also the Rectory and church of Chaddesley, in the county of Worcester, with all its rights, members, and appurtenances, to the said late college of St Mary, in the said town of Warwick, lately belonging and appertaining; and also the Rectory and church of Budebroke, in the County of Warwick, with all its rights, members and appurtenances, to the same late college of St Mary in the said town of Warwick lately belonging and appertaining; and also the advowsons, donations, presentations, free dispositions, rights of patronage of the vicarages and churches of St Mary, St Nicholas, Budebroke, in the county of Warwick and of the vicarage and church of Chaddesley, in the county of Worcester, to the said late college, lately belonging and appertaining; and also a messuage, house, and tenement, with the appurtenances, in a street called Cannon-row in the said town of Warwick, late in the occupation of David Vaughan, clerk, or his assigns; and also all houses, edifices, stables, gardens, grounds, orchards, lands, hereditaments, etc. in the said street called Cannon-row, with the said messuage demised and to the same late college lately belonging; and the said king also granted to the said Burgesses all his messuages, houses, edifices, lands, tenements, rents, reservations, services, woods, glebes, tithes, pensions, portions, fruits, emoluments etc. and heriditaments whatever, with their appurtenances, as well spiritual as temporal, situated and being, coming, growing, and renewing in the towns, fields, parishes, and hamlets of Warwick, Chaddesley, and Budebroke, or in any of them, in the said counties of Warwick and Worcester or elsewhere wheresoever in the same counties ... ... at the clear yearly value of £58 14sh 4d."

In simple terms this meant that the Burgesses were granted the churches of St Mary, St Nicholas, Budbrooke and Chaddesley Corbett, together with various houses, lands and rights , such as tithes, belonging to these churches.

In return the Burgesses had to pay various stipends including the vicar of St Mary's £20 annually, The vicar of St Nicholas £13 6sh 8d, the vicar of Budbrooke £5 3sh 4d together with other payments to the Bishop and Archdeacon of Worcester and £6 13sh 4d to the crown.

St Mary's Collegiate church had maintained the Grammar School, so the Burgesses were to take responsibility for the school and pay a salary of £10 p.a. to the schoolmaster.

The Guild of Warwick

As the Guild played such a crucial role it is necessary to understand something of its history.

Guilds generally had been set up to look after the interests of their members and privileges were granted by the Crown and local over-lords (e.g. the Earls of Warwick) such as the right to buy and sell within the town without paying a toll. In Warwick two Guilds had been formed in 1383 ... St George the Martyr and Holy Trinity and St Mary. Between 1392 and 1415 they had amalgamated into the United Guild of Warwick. Amongst other things the Guild supplied priests to sing masses for the souls of the dead in St James' Chapel over Westgate and in St Peter's Chapel over Eastgate. The amalgamated Guild had had a Banqueting Hall constructed around 1383 near Westgate, and a Guildhall for private business meetings, was built around 1450 by Neville "The Kingmaker" Earl of Warwick.

The Guild of Warwick was a powerful body which owned various other properties besides its official buildings.

When the Charter provided for the Burgesses to administer the town, it was the members of the Common Council of the Guild who became the Burgesses and thus the same body of men retained power, only their title was different. As E.G. Tibbits pointed out ... many other towns had property restored to them, but Warwick was very fortunate because continuity was not lost.

Long before the Guilds themselves were officially abolished in 1548, the Guild of Warwick transferred to the Charity of King Henry VIII its remaining properties and obligations. Thus the Corporation became responsible for such items as maintenance of the Great Bridge, but in return had acquired an annual sum of around £11 from the former Guild Estate.

1554 Charter of Queen Mary.

By 1554 there were some problems which needed clarification and a further charter gave the Corporation more powers and income.

In the Charter dated 12th November 1554 the inhabitants of Warwick were re-incorporated as "The Bailiff and Burgesses of the Borough of Warwick in the County of Warwick" and the Common Council was to consist of a Bailiff (Mayor) and 12 Burgesses (Aldermen) who were elected for life. The Corporation also consisted of 12 Assistant Burgesses and the Inhabitant Burgesses who were those who paid Church and Poor Rates. When one of the Aldermen died, a new Alderman was chosen by the others and the Assistant Burgesses were also chosen by the Bailiff and Aldermen.

In 1554 the Booth Hall and market tolls were granted to the Corporation and the profits from these were to constitute "The Bailiff's Account" which was supposed to be used for civic entertaining.

It also provided for a Recorder, to be in charge of law and order, a Deputy Recorder (Town Clerk), Clerk of the Market, Sergeant at Mace, Yeoman and Beadle. Part of Bailiff's duties had been to oversee the affairs of the weekly market and he had also been the chief Magistrate, presiding over the weekly court. Although prestigious, the position of Bailiff had not been popular with some and in fact some Burgesses, having been elected as Bailiff, made excuses or refused to serve and were fined.

The Dudley Family

The activities of the Corporation in the 16th century were very much bound up with the influential Dudley family, who as powerful local Lords caused the Burgesses of Warwick a great deal of expense.

John Dudley (the son of Edmund Dudley the tax inspector of King Henry VII whom King Henry VIII had had executed) was a talented ambitious schemer and King Henry VIII used him as an effective administrator. Until the death of King Henry VIII Warwick Castle remained Crown property, but when Edward VI came to the throne in 1547 he created John Dudley Earl of Warwick. In 1551 Dudley was created Duke of Northumberland, but within 2 years he had been beheaded for treason. He influenced King Edward VI to sign a patent naming Lady Jane Grey, the wife of his son Guildford Dudley, as the next monarch and when Edward died, Northumberland proclaimed Jane as Queen because as a Protestant he wished to exclude Catholic Mary Tudor (the eldest daughter of King Henry VIII) from the succession. However the Dudleys' plot failed and Lady Jane, her husband Guildford Dudley and the Duke of Northumberland were all executed.

In Warwick there were some, notably Thomas Fisher, who had acted as agent for John Dudley who had subsequently become very wealthy. He bought the Priory in Warwick, which he rebuilt, and there can be no doubt that in this period, an atmosphere of bribery and great uncertainty, assisted by the presence of numerous spies, blighted the lives of honest citizens.

John Dudley's body was buried, complete with its severed head, in the Tower of London in St Peter's Church, close by the remains of two of King Henry VIII's wives, Anne Boleyn and Catherine Howard, both of whom had been beheaded some years before.

Ambrose Dudley (son of the powerful John) was imprisoned for his part in the Lady Jane Grey Plot, but he was later released and created Earl of Warwick in 1561 by Queen Elizabeth I. He became a great favourite of the Queen as did his brother Robert and it was during this period that Queen Elizabeth paid several visits to the area, sometimes staying at Warwick Castle. Ambrose and his brother Robert, Earl of Leycester, caused the Corporation of Warwick much expense from the Charity of King Henry VIII as the Corporation felt obliged to offer to their lordships various presents. For example in 1571 they were given a yoke of oxen apiece which cost around £10. Ambrose was generally known as "The Good Earl" because of his pleasant disposition, but he was one of the nobles who sat in judgement at Fotheringay at the trial of Mary Queen of Scots.

In his youth he had been wounded in the leg and later in life repeated trouble from the leg led to amputation and eventually death in London in 1590. He was buried in The Beauchamp Chapel in St Mary's Warwick... his stone tomb being adorned with various heraldic devices associated with the Dudley family.

Robert, the younger brother of Ambrose, was the favourite courtier and possibly the lover of Queen Elizabeth I. He was frequently to be found at the Queen's side and naturally she heaped honours upon him.

*THIS INTELLIGENT,
ATHLETIC YET
RATHER VAIN MAN
WAS A CLOSE
FRIEND, POSSIBLY
THE LOVER, OF
QUEEN ELIZABETH
I. Robert Dudley (1533
to 1588), Earl of
Leycester, was for many
years one of the most
influential men in
England and he had
many connections with
Warwick and the
Charity of King Henry
VIII. This portrait by
an unknown artist was
painted around 1575.
(By courtesy of the
National Portrait
Gallery, London)*

In 1562 he was granted the then magnificent Kenilworth Castle, where he entertained the Queen on several occasions and he was later created Earl of Leycester. It was said that his parliamentary influence was enormous and certainly the Burgesses of Warwick did not care to annoy him, so in 1571 they allowed him to have the former Guild property near Westgate to found his hospital for old soldiers.

His romances and marriages were full of intrigue and it was rumoured that he had murdered his first wife Amy Robsart. There is a piece of her needlework on display today in the Brethren's Kitchen of the Lord Leycester Hospital and many visitors are fascinated. Leycester's second wife was Lady Sheffield who bore him a son, but later he married widow Lettice Knowlls, Countess of Essex, many alleged bigamously. Their son, known as "The Noble Imp", died whilst still a small child and was buried in the Beauchamp Chapel, and his tiny suit of armour can still be seen in the Great Hall of Warwick Castle. As for Robert Dudley himself, he died in 1589 and was buried in the Beauchamp Chapel. His widow Lettice (detested by Queen Elizabeth?) survived him for 40 years; soon after Leycester's death she had married a much younger man Christopher Blount, but in 1601 he was executed. Eventually Lettice died in 1634 at the age of 92 "On Christmas Day in the morning" as her memorial reads and she was buried alongside Leycester in the Beauchamp Chapel.

I must confess that in common with many others I find the huge tomb of Robert Dudley very unattractive, but I suppose it was in keeping with his 'larger than life' character.

The Black Book of Warwick

The Black Book is a wonderful handwritten volume giving details of many events which concerned the Corporation of Warwick and the ways in which King Henry VIII Charity money was spent. Largely written by John Fisher a prominent man who was Bailiff 1564/5 and 1580/81, Town Clerk for many years and sometime Member of Parliament for Warwick, the Black Book is mostly about the years 1563-1590 although other people added to it afterwards.

The various members of the Fisher family are interesting as they illustrate how it was possible for lower born people to climb to positions of eminence, with the patronage of wealthy lords. Their family name was really Hawkins, but it is said that John, Richard and Thomas adopted the name of Fisher because their father had sold fish in the market place.

The transcription of The Black Book made by Alderman Thomas Kemp in 1898 is easy to read and there are sub-headings to help identify sections. In this volume I have insufficient space to include many of the interesting tales told about the Corporation, but those fascinated by the details of history can read the book for themselves. Also John Fisher compiled a second volume "The Book of John Fisher" which although much smaller, gives many contemporary details, invaluable to today's historians.

The Corporation Lose the Guildhall Premises

In 1571 the Earl of Leycester decided that he wanted to found a hospital for old soldiers where they could live after they had finished serving their queen and country ... possibly to please the Queen. An approach was made to the Corporation of Warwick as he decided that the Guildhall premises, complete with the adjoining Westgate and Chapel of St James would be ideal for his purpose. Not unnaturally the Corporation was not keen to give away their premises, but the Earl tried to put pressure on the members saying that he would go to Kenilworth instead, if they did not agree. Only Thomas Oken, by then a very old man, dared to point out the usefulness of the buildings which he felt the Corporation would be unwise to give away. Oken had already signed his complicated will, leaving his money to the town for a variety of civic purposes and there was not much the Earl of Leycester or anyone else could do to harm him.

IMAGINE A GROUP OF INFLUENTIAL WARWICK MEN, DRESSED IN RUFFLES, DOUBLETS AND HOSE, HAVING A HUGE ROW NEAR THESE SAME STAIRS, SHOUTING, SWEARING AND SPITTING IN SOMEONE'S FACE. It actually happened on 17th December 1564 when an Assistant Burgess named Powell "swore by God's blood and other grait othes" that the Bailiff and Burgesses had mismanaged the revenues of King Henry VIH's Charity. The Black Book of Warwick carried a very amusing account of the row near the Guildhall (now part of the Lord Leycester Hospital). (JF)

However the Earl got his way; the Corporation granted him the buildings provided that he found them alternative accommodation for the Grammar School and the Corporation meetings. The Earls of Warwick and Leycester promised the town St Peter's Chapel above Eastgate for use by the school and the Cross Tavern (on the site of the present Court House) and the Shire Hall was given for Corporation Meetings and Civic events. However money to restore these buildings was not granted until 1576 and only then after repeated requests from John Fisher and others.

Oken's Charity

In 1573 Thomas Oken died leaving his considerable wealth to a charity bearing his name, which in various capacities was to benefit the town. In many respects there seemed to be deliberate overlap with the Charity of King Henry VIII, especially in respect of money to repair the Great Bridge and certain roads. For much of the time since 1545 the income from the Charity of King Henry VIII was insufficient for the civic expenditure and Oken seemed to be such a public spirited

OKEN'S HOUSE IN CASTLE STREET NOW HOUSES THE FAMOUS DOLL AND TOY MUSEUM. With Guy's Tower of Warwick Castle visible behind, the reason for the name of the street on the left, which once led past the Castle to the former Great Bridge, is apparent. This photograph was taken in late 1993, but it has become difficult to photograph old buildings without road signs, traffic or crowds of people obscuring the view. (JF)

THIS WONDERFUL OAK CHEST IN THE COURT HOUSE IS THOUGHT TO HAVE BELONGED TO THOMAS OKEN AND IS DATED 1573. There are nine separate locks because in previous centuries multi-lock chests (with a different key for each Trustee) were considered safer. Appropriately King Henry VIII's Charity gave a grant towards restoration work in 1988. (Photograph by Simon Photography, Warwick)

individual that he thought of the poor and many essential services in his will. There were some in Warwick who did not wish him to leave so much to charity and Page 184 of The Black Book gives graphic details of how, as the old man lay dying, some tried to revive him by shouting and rubbing his body, in order that he might be persuaded to change his will.

It must be stressed that today Oken's Charity is an entirely separate charity from King Henry VIII's, administered by a separate body of Trustees, but in the past this was not always the case. Although Oken left precise instructions for the administering of his estate, in practice members of the Corporation were the Trustees and there were many areas where the two charities overlapped. I believe this could have been deliberate policy by Oken who might have thought that public money would be safer if coming from separate sources, so that even if the Crown interfered with one source, the other might still remain.

Amongst other things Oken left money for the repair of the Great Bridge, Emscote Bridge, the Common Wells, Wedgnock Lane and other roads besides £2 annually to the schoolmaster of the Grammar School (Warwick School) and £2 annually to a teacher of poor men's children (perhaps in a revival of the old Choir School at St Mary's). From 1700 this sum was granted to the master of the Bablake Charity School held over Eastgate.

Amongst the many other bequests in Oken's will were payments to the Beadle and other town officials, payments for the poor and provision for almshouses and directions for an annual feast, intended as a revival of the Guild Feast. This feast is still held each year on the last Friday in January, in the form that Thomas Oken directed, preceded by a service in St Mary's attended by Trustees and local dignitaries. The toast to Thomas Oken and his wife Joan is repeated every year and the founder of modern Warwick is suitably remembered.

INSTANTLY RECOGNISABLE, THIS DRAWING FROM THE AYLESFORD COLLECTION SHOWS THE ALMSHOUSES ON CASTLE HILL AS THEY WERE IN 1821. In 1994 the 10 apartments (belonging to Oken's and Eyffler's Charities) underwent major restoration with modern kitchens and bathrooms being added. King Henry VIII's Charity made a grant towards this major project. When I visited, John the foreman told me of how a 1764 Auction List of Warwick Ironmongers, F. W. Holmes, was found under a floorboard, but sadly the paper disintegrated. (Reproduced by permission of Birmingham City Archives)

OKEN'S FEAST IS CELEBRATED EVERY YEAR AT THE END OF JANUARY AND THIS PHOTOGRAPH WAS TAKEN AT THE CELEBRATION IN THE LORD LEYCESTER HOSPITAL IN 1993. Thomas Oken left many charitable bequests in his will (dated 1571) amongst them money and silver items for a revival of the former Guild feast. From the left is Rev. Steven Little (Team Rector of the Parish of Warwick); Ralph Thornton (Chairman of Oken's Trustees); Michael Gaffney (Town Clerk); Lady Benson (Guest of Honour); Councillor Neil Thurley (Mayor of Warwick) and Terence Horn (Clerk of Oken's Charity). (Photograph courtesy of Leamington Spa Courier)

The Visit of Queen Elizabeth I in 1572

As Queen Elizabeth was so fond of Ambrose and Robert Dudley, the Earls of Warwick and Leycester, she paid several visits to the Warwick area.

Her second visit in August 1572 is described at length in The Black Book and it makes fascinating reading. Attended by numerous Lords and Ladies including Lord Burghley, The Earl of Sussex, Lord Howard of Effingham, the Earl of Oxford, the Earl of Warwick and her favourite Earl of Leycester, the Queen dined en route at the house of Edward Fisher at Bishop's Itchington. Edward was the son of Thomas Fisher, one time agent of John Dudley and the owner of the Priory in Warwick.

Instead of proceeding to Warwick by the usual route in those times via Tachbrook and the Myton Fields, the Queen's party was diverted through Chesterton Pastures and by Oakley because the former road was bad as the weather had "bene very fowle long tyme before". Even in those days the August weather could be wet! So the welcoming party from Warwick, instead of meeting her majesty at the gate between Tachbrook Field and Myton Field had to divert quickly to Ford Mill Hill (now enclosed within the Castle Park) where they greeted the queen in order … first the Bailiff, then the Recorder, then the Principal Burgesses … all kneeling. It was about 3 o'clock and after the Recorder had made a long welcoming speech, the Bailiff presented Queen Elizabeth with a purse "very faire wrought" containing £20 in gold sovereigns. The queen smiled and made a few protestations about not expecting gifts each time she came, but she graciously accepted the purse all the same! Throughout the ceremonies the town mace was resting in the queen's lap, where she had placed it after the Bailiff had formally presented it, but after Rafe Griffin the schoolmaster had given the queen some latin verses (which she handed over to Lady Warwick who was riding with her in the coach) the town party rode "two & two together" to Warwick Castle at the head of the queen's procession.

Later in the visit there was a mock battle enacted by means of fireworks during which many "fire balles & squibbes" were fired into the air, some of them falling in the town. A number of houses were damaged, an elderly couple asleep in their

QUEEN ELIZABETH I (SHOWN HERE IN A PAINTING OF 1575 BY AN UNKNOWN ARTIST) VISITED WARWICK FOR THE SECOND TIME ON 12TH AUGUST 1572. The Queen and her large entourage arrived at Ford Mill Hill (now enclosed in the Castle Park) around 3 p.m. to be met by the Bailiff Robert Philipps, the Recorder Mr Aglionby and senior members of the Corporation. A purse containing twenty sovereigns was presented to her by the Bailiff on behalf of the town. (By courtesy of the National Portrait Gallery, London)

house near the Great Bridge had a very narrow escape when their house was burnt down and it seems amazing that there was no major tragedy.

This show was supposedly paid for by the Earl of Warwick, but the Town of Warwick presented him with a fat ox and 10 sheep to help with the food. Although not primarily responsible for the entertaining of important visitors, there can be little doubt that royal visits such as that of Queen Elizabeth I gave the Corporation huge financial problems. There was insufficient surplus profit from the Charity of King Henry VIII to pay for even modest civic entertaining or gifts.

The Enormous Influence of the Earl

When researching this subject, only gradually did the huge power of the Earls of Warwick dawn on me.

From around 1600 Sir Fulke Greville was appointed Recorder, long before he was granted the Castle and Sir Fulke was only the first of many holders of the title Lord

GEORGE 2ND EARL (1773 TO 1816) BUILT THE NEW CASTLE BRIDGE IN 1793 AND ENCLOSED A SIZABLE SECTION OF THE TOWN WITHIN THE CASTLE WALLS. He spent much time and money improving the Castle itself and purchased many of the valuable paintings and furnishings on view there today. He had many negotiations with the Corporation and his actions had a huge effect on the town and its finances. (Photograph by courtesy of Warwick Castle)

Brooke (or Earl of Warwick) to be appointed Recorder, and the Recorder had the power to appoint the Deputy Recorder (Town Clerk) who wielded a great deal of power. Also the Earl had great influence when the choice of Aldermen came up and it was this which ensured that the Earl always had his way. The Aldermen and the Bailiff (later Mayor) often ruled without Assistant Burgesses whom they were supposed to consult, and when it came to the election of Members of Parliament the Earl's nominees were almost always elected. Thus it could be argued that the Earls of Warwick in fact, if not on paper, had great control over how the revenue of King Henry VIII's Charity was spent. If a project for public good displeased the Earl, it was unlikely to be adopted. From time to time, various influential people tried to break the dominance of the Earl, but they met with limited success.

Rulers of the Castle who were Recorders of the town were Robert 2nd Baron Brooke 1628-1643, Robert Lord Brooke 1641-3, Francis 3rd Baron Brooke 1643-1658, Robert Lord Brooke 1659-76, Fulke Greville Lord Brooke 1676-1710, Hon. Doddington Greville, Lord Brooke 1711-1719, William Lord Brooke 1719-1727, Rt Hon. Francis Brooke, Earl of Warwick from 1759, Recorder from 1741-1773, George Earl of Warwick 1773-1816, Henry Earl of Warwick 1816-1835. After this time, the Recorder had to be a Barrister at Law of at least 5 years' standing.

Subsequent charters which modified the Corporation law were made by James I in 1612, Charles II in 1664 and 1684 and William and Mary in 1694.

In addition to these there were various decrees of Chancery which modified the ways in which the money from King Henry VIII's Charity was spent.

The Seventeenth Century

By inviting Sir Fulke Greville to be the Recorder around 1600 the Corporation incurred the wrath of Lord Leigh of Stoneleigh who had hoped for the position himself. So he alleged that the Corporation had misappropriated the income from King Henry VIII's Charity and the result was Lord Ellsmere's Decree in 1615. By this decree, the stipends of the clergy and the school master were substantially increased ... the vicar of St Mary's was increased from £20 to £60 and the schoolmaster from £10 to £20. Also the accounts had to be submitted for scrutiny to the Sheriff for the County of Warwickshire and Lord Leigh held that position himself.

By now the value of the original charity had resulted in a large increase in income and in 1637 Lord Keeper Coventry's Decree resulted in more increases in salaries. Also this decree was more long ranging than others as it stipulated that money was to given to the poor of the town and used for apprenticing needy persons. The accounts were to be kept in a more detailed manner and not only the chancel, but also the church of St Mary was to be kept in repair.

Royal Visits by King James and King Charles Bankrupt the Town.

In 1545 when King Henry VIII's Charity was first set up the annual income was nearly £80. When money from the previous Guild account and other sources had been taken into account there was an average income for the years between 1545 and 1569 of £97. From "The Book of John Fisher" we learn that average expenditure in this period was nearly £87 p.a. The Corporation only had to grant some expensive presents to the Earl or Monarch and they became heavily in debt.

Such a situation was when on 4th September 1617 King James I was entertained in the former Guild Banqueting Hall by the Corporation and Sir Fulke Greville, who was then in the process of restoring Warwick Castle which could not be used. Michael Harryot, then Bailiff, actually loaned money for expenses, but several years later, he had still not been repaid as the Corporation had insufficient income to pay its debts.

In 1636 Charles I paid a visit to the town and not only was the king given a gift of a gilt cup which altogether, with the cost of an inscription and a presentation box, cost £21 10sh 10d. but also his numerous retainers expected a gratuity too. The list as given by Thomas Kemp in his "History of Warwick and Its People" included 20 different categories of retainers including footmen who received 40 shillings, coachmen 10 shillings, even the jester who also received 10 shillings.

KING JAMES I VISITED WARWICK IN 1617 AND WAS ENTERTAINED IN THE BANQUETING HALL AT THE LORD LEYCESTER HOSPITAL. Royal visits put a huge strain on the Corporation budgets as profits from King Henry VIII's Estate were barely sufficient for normal expenditure. The poor Bailiff in 1617 Michael Harryot had to supplement Corporation funds himself because the king was "right nobly entertained at supper". King James I is shown here in a painting of 1621 by Daniel Mytens. (By courtesy of the National Portrait Gallery, London)

IN AUGUST 1636 KING CHARLES I (SHOWN IN AN UNDATED PORTRAIT BY DANIEL MYTENS) VISITED WARWICK AND WAS THE GUEST OF LORD BROOKE AT THE CASTLE. However the Corporation also spent a vast amount of money in receiving the king. They bought him an expensive gilt cup which cost over £21 and his numerous retainers were given gifts of money. Ironically a few years later Lord Brooke was fighting against the king during the Civil War and Warwick Castle was successfully held for the Parliamentarians. (By courtesy of the National Portrait Gallery, London)

Altogether payments to the various retainers amounted to £35 and the king's visit cost the Corporation a vast amount. The Corporation did not have enough money so it was recorded that Alderman George Weale brought £100 from his son John to lend to the Borough and a guarantee bond of £200 was made, sealed with the Common Seal of the Corporation.

The Civil War, the Restoration and the Bloodless Revolution

As Robert the 2nd Lord Brooke was an ardent supporter of the Parliamentary cause in the Civil War, Warwick Castle was spared any destruction in the years of conflict between 1642 and 1651. The Castle did survive a minor siege by Royalist forces in 1642 but apart from that saw little serious action. However on 14th June 1642 the town suffered damage from Parliamentary troops, under the command of a local Puritan Colonel Purefoy. William Purefoy of Caldecot Hall near Nuneaton had been elected as M.P. for Warwick in 1640 because of the influence of Lord Brooke and in the Civil War had become a colonel.

The fanatical soldiers, urged on by William Purefoy, entered the Beauchamp Chapel in St Mary's and did a huge amount of damage as they regarded the Chantry Chapel as a place signifying Roman Catholic ideals and therefore evil. They smashed the priceless windows and the magnificent altar, leaving the Corporation in an awkward position as the general care of St Mary's was part of their responsibility. Not content with damaging the chapel, Colonel Purefoy then supervised the destruction of the Market Cross which stood in the Market Place.

Robert the 2nd Lord Brooke was killed in the Battle of Lichfield in 1643 and his successor, his son Francis, 3rd Lord Brooke, also supported the Parliamentary cause. Later Colonel Purefoy became one of the commissioners who signed the Death Warrant of King Charles I in 1649.

Robert Greville, 4th Lord Brooke became a Royalist and played a prominent part in the Restoration in 1660, but some members of the Corporation had problems. In 1662 several members including Thomas Crane the Bailiff and fellow Puritans Robert Heath and Richard Ainge felt they could not take the oath of allegiance to King Charles II so they were evicted from office.

In the years that followed other Burgesses had trouble with their official duties and this helped to swell the Corporation coffers. In 1674/5 all the Assistant Burgesses were fined 3 shillings for neglecting their duties and they had to pay a further 4d each Sunday they neglected to attend St Mary's Church in their gowns, … which they were obliged to do by the charter.

When James II came to the throne in 1685 he arrogantly tried to interfere with Government, furthering the Roman Catholic cause wherever possible. He attempted to exert control over town Corporations and Warwick was no exception. In 1687 Rev. Eades was appointed vicar of St Mary's, but the Corporation suspected him of being sympathetic to Catholics and they tried to oust him. The town was deprived of its charter and soldiers were sometimes quartered in the town as a warning.

Fearing that the king was about to interfere with the governing of Warwick, on 7th August 1688 the Corporation voted to place the revenues of the Charity of King Henry VIII in the hands of Trustees, nominating the men then Corporation members, so that the king could not get access to the money. Their fears were justified and on 26th August 1688 King James II suspended the Corporation by Royal Warrant, substituting men who supported the Catholic cause in their place.

However King James was forced to flee the country when the "Bloodless Revolution" took place in the autumn of 1688 and the old Corporation resumed their former positions in December. Until a new charter was granted several years later, they had no legal right to do so as later Acts of Parliament had not covered Warwick.

A New Charter and a Fire in 1694

Following "The Bloodless Revolution" of 1688 William and Mary became the next sovereigns and as Warwick still had no charter, another was sought. Protestant Mary was the daughter of King James II's first marriage to Anne Hyde and William, also a Protestant, had a good claim to the throne himself. Both were acceptable to the majority of citizens of Warwick, although there did seem to be many in the town who had supported James and the Jacobite cause.

In 1690 Rev. Eades of St Mary's was publicly accused by various members of the Corporation of attending the consecration in 1689 of a new Roman Catholic Chapel in the Saltisford. Dr Johnson (from 1692 the owner of Landor House), James Fish the Parish Clerk of St Mary's and his son James Fish the younger, the famous surveyor, were also implicated and they might have been some of the "closet Jacobites" in Warwick who found worship in St Mary's acceptable because it still retained many of the trappings of Catholicism.

The Royal Warwickshire Regiment also began at this time, being in its early days composed of mercenaries fighting for William of Orange, hence the fact that the colours of the regiment are those of the Dutch Royal Household. The influence of the Puritan Earls in the 17th century helped to make Warwick very anti-Catholic.

Until the new Charter was signed, William Tarver as previous Mayor was asked to continue, but it made the administration of King Henry VIII's Charity far easier when the new Charter was obtained. Presumably life in those times in Warwick was very troubled as on 5th September 1694 a terrible fire destroyed or damaged 250 of the 600 houses in the town. The fire began in High Street, opposite to the Lord Leycester Hospital and even St Mary's Church was destroyed, although fortunately not the chancel or Beauchamp Chapel. Obviously with a disaster of that magnitude, the Corporation could not cope without financial assistance and a disaster fund was set up which had donations from many sources. The fact that the Beauchamp Chapel escaped seemed to be largely due to James Fish, the Parish Clerk of St Mary's and a gang of firefighters who stopped the fire at the doorway to the chapel. In 1700 local mason Samuel Dunkley carved the present doorway, as much like the other as possible. Queen Anne contributed money to the restoration and her monogram can be seen in several places.

The Corporation Lose Control of King Henry VIII's Charity

The Charter of 1694 ordered that every Michaelmas Day, the Mayor and Alderman in the presence of the Burgesses should choose two Aldermen (neither of whom had served as Mayor for the past two years) and from them choose one to be the next Mayor. However correct procedures were not always followed and in the early decades of the eighteenth century, the Corporation seemed do exactly as they pleased. A new Court House was begun on the site of the old Cross Tavern at the corner of Castle Street and Jury Street because although the old building survived the Great Fire, it was not in good repair. Francis Smith, an Alderman and past Mayor, designed and built the elegant building, but there was insufficient income from the Charity of King Henry VIII to pay for it and large debts were incurred.

Many of the opponents of the Corporation in Warwick were members of the Whig Party who stood for reform and wished to lessen the power of the Earl, especially concerning the way in which the Members of Parliament were elected. At that time, Warwick returned two Members, almost always the Tory nominees of the Earl. Very few men had the vote and it was largely the Earl through the Corporation who decided matters.

In 1734 wealthy Thomas Archer of Umberslade and his brother Henry forced an election to be held to select the Members of Parliament for Warwick. The Earl's Tory nominees were usually adopted unopposed but the Archer brothers, both Whig supporters were victorious, despite bribery by the Tory Mayor. In 1735 the Archers and several others then alleged that there had been gross misappropriation of money and in 1741 the Corporation had the running of King Henry VIII's Estate taken from them. It would have been difficult to directly challenge the power of the Castle, but it was possible to appeal to Chancery concerning the misapplication of the town's finances. So the financial complaint was the instrument of lessening the power of the Corporation and thereby the Earl.

An enquiry stated that the Corporation had debts of over £4,000 and as the members were unable to pay this huge sum, an official Receiver was appointed to run the finances of the town. Not until 1769 did the Corporation succeed in regaining control of King Henry VIII's Estate. Undoubtedly there had been corruption and some poor decisions made but I had to smile when I read what E.G. Tibbits had written about this.

"… it seems that this melancholy state of affairs was brought by lethargy and mismanagement rather than by deliberate corruption."

After the Corporation resumed control, for a time, Dr Walter Landor (the father of the poet Walter Savage Landor) led an Independent Party seeking political reform which succeeded in forcing an election in 1774 which resulted in the election of one Whig M.P. for Warwick. This was the first election since 1734 but real reforms were few and far between and what was happening in Warwick was also happening elsewhere.

The Nineteenth Century

In 1826 proceedings were taken against the Mayor and some of the Aldermen for not holding the Mayoral election properly.

John Wilmshurst had just been elected for his 3rd successive year and it was felt that reform of Corporation practice was long overdue. In the last thirty years, two men had been Mayor for 7 consecutive years and protectionism and corruption were rife. From 1792-1799 Charles Gregory Wade had been Mayor, having previously been Mayor in 1786/7 and John Bohun Smyth had been Mayor from 1811 till his death in 1819. It was a similar story in many places in England and complacency and bad practice were soon to be swept away in the aftermath of the passing of The Reform Bill in 1832.

1835 ONWARDS

The Municipal Corporations Act of 1835 meant an end to the old style Corporation in Warwick whereby the town had been ruled by a Mayor and twelve Aldermen, selected for life. From 1835 on, local power was given to an elected body of men who served for a fixed term, similar to the system in use today.

Long before Domesday, the Earls of Warwick (or the major landowners in possession of Warwick Castle) had had an enormous influence on the town and this had continued for centuries. It seems likely that directly or indirectly, the Earls had effectively controlled almost all the activities of the town. In earlier centuries, none dared oppose the nobleman, even if he was an unscrupulous man oblivious to the ghastly lives led by many of the poorer inhabitants of the town. In the later 18th century, some powerful local men such as Dr Walter Landor (father of the poet Walter Savage Landor)and Samuel Parr (the scholarly curate of Hatton) had tried to limit the power of the Castle, especially in the choice of Members of Parliament, but bribery and fear had bolstered the Earl's cause. Many of the Earls had been typical feudal rulers and no worse than other members of the upper class in a class-ridden society. However the lives of most inhabitants were improved when power was vested in an elected body, over which the Castle had a limited influence.

From 1835 onwards the town council of six Aldermen and 18 Councillors was chosen by ratepayers, but in those times only around 1,000 men were eligible to vote. The Whigs (reforming party) had largely been excluded in the old Council, but in 1835 all the Aldermen and most of the Councillors belonged to the Whig Party. As time went on, instead of the Council being largely composed of professional men, there were an increasing number of tradesmen, shopkeepers and private residents elected.

The 'knock on' effect of the famous Reform Act of 1832 and the Municipal Corporations Act of 1835 meant the passing of the Municipal Charities Act of 1836. For the very first time the running of King Henry VIII's Charity and the other town charities was taken from Warwick Corporation and placed in the hands of officially nominated Trustees ... a separate body of men nominated by the Lord Chancellor for the duration of their life-time.

The Municipal Charity Trustees

As might be expected, the Tory Party, backed by the Earl and members of his family, wished to hold on to power in respect of the important charities of Warwick. In 1835 the first elected Council in Warwick was composed almost entirely of members of the Whig Party (only 2 Tories) and on 16th August 1836 the Whig Mayor, William Collins, made an official petition to the Lord Chancellor that 17 men (15 Whig Councillors, 1 Tory Councillor and 1 other Whig) might be appointed as the new Trustees for the Municipal Charities. On 20th August 1836 a second petition was presented to the Lord Chancellor this time from John Wilmshurst (a surgeon) and three others which suggested that 11 men, all members of the former Tory Corporation might be Trustees. A further complication was that James Tibbits, the Tory Town Clerk, (aged only 22 when appointed by the old Tory Corporation) presented a petition of his own suggesting 12 Whigs and 12 Tories.

Eventually in September 1836, 21 Municipal Charity Trustees were chosen …16 Whigs from the Mayor's Petition and 5 Tories from the other petitions.

The Whig Council, who had only endorsed the appointment of James Tibbits as Town Clerk because they thought it would be too costly to pay him compensation for loss of office, were furious and dismissed him anyway. A Whig, Thomas Heath (father of R.C. Heath) was appointed in place of James Tibbits, but a great deal of trouble was caused for the Council as a result.

James Tibbits became Chairman of the local Conservative Association and was elected to the Council in 1837. However the Whig Mayor tried to eliminate him on a technicality and James Tibbits then won a battle in the High Court forcing his election to stand and claiming heavy compensation from the Whig Council. Costs were awarded against the Council and for several years a large slice of the income of King Henry VIII's Charity went to pay the lengthy Chancery proceedings. James Tibbits went from strength to strength and by 1840, largely because of the trouble he had caused for Thomas Heath and other Liberals, there was a Tory majority on the Council. James Tibbits then resumed the office of Town Clerk and never again did the Whigs, or Liberals as they later became known, have a majority on the Town Council in the 19th century.

The Trustees of the Municipal Charities in the 19th Century

The Trustees first met on 11th November 1836 with the Mayor Charles Lamb as Chairman. The row between Whigs and Tories continued in meetings as the Whig majority appointed Whig Thomas Heydon as the Official Receiver of Rents etc. The previous Receiver of the Charity had been Tory George Greenway and when he lost the office, he refused for several years to hand over the necessary documents connected with the charity.

After a struggle, the Municipal Trustees gave up Oken's Charity, which should have been separate anyway but it took a number of years to sort out the muddle.

Basically it transpired that once the salaries had been paid and any necessary repairs and bills paid, the surplus from the profits of King Henry VIII's Charity was to be handed over to the newly created Borough Fund, which paid for the town's expenses. In other words, the profits of King Henry VIII's Charity subsidised the Borough Rates.

In 1838 the first Borough Rate of $1^1/_2$d (0.6p) in the pound was imposed to help pay for a new gaol and engine house. The Borough Rate was collected in each parish by the churchwardens and overseers and although in the early years the collection was rather haphazard gradually the system improved.

On Lady Day 1837 £1,750 was transferred to the Borough Fund as being the balance of income from King Henry VIII's estate and from then on each year the surplus income was similarly passed on. In 1843 this income was £750 but by 1872 it had risen to £2,364.

In 1835 the Council had formed a Watch Committee to supervise the police force, fire service, street lighting, and the management of prisoners but in 1840 the Trustees of King Henry VIII's Charity decided that they would not be responsible any longer for gas lighting of streets or for the police. There was a difficult situation but the bizarre result was that 13 members of the Council were appointed to help administer Oken's Charity, which then took over the payments for the Watch Committee.

The large increase in the population of Warwick in the nineteenth century (from 5,592 in 1801 to 11,903 in 1891) meant that new water supplies and drainage schemes were urgently needed. In 1843 a Waterworks Scheme was implemented and in 1847 the Council formed a Public Health Committee. In 1850 the Public Health Committee was enlarged to cover highways, drainage and sanitation. 1876 saw the formation of an Education Committee and 1878 a Sewage Committee. By 1919 there were 11 Committees including a Free Library Committee. The profits from King Henry VIII's Charity continued to be handed over to the Town Council to help finance such schemes.

The latter part of the nineteenth century saw many changes in Warwick as elsewhere and King Henry VIII's Charity gradually became less important, as Borough Rates were collected more effectively and supplied a greater part of the finance.

Older Properties. An Era of Change?

As with all older properties in an age of great change, there was constant pressure to adapt and modernise ageing buildings which had been built to accommodate the simpler demands of earlier centuries. The old College Building in The Butts, then the home of the Grammar School, was a good example and when Rev. Herbert Hill was appointed headmaster in 1843 a great deal of work was done on the buildings. St Peter's Chapel above Eastgate had been used to house the Bablake Charity School which was funded from several educational charities. However during the 19th century, the building needed repairs and extensions to accommodate the growing number of pupils.

The burning question of the later half of the 19th century was education and nationwide it was realised that drastic changes had to be made. Of all the changes which had beset King Henry VIII Charity, none was so great as when the King's Schools Foundation was set up.

Since 1545 the responsibility for the running of the Grammar School had rested with King Henry VIII's Charity, but now urgent, extra funds were necessary for new buildings and general modernisation of the curriculum. All the charities in Warwick were invited to contribute, not only those concerned with education, and it was pointed out that the best way to help the poor was to educate their children. Victorian morality was often harsh and several charities which had existed for centuries to assist the poor were swallowed up by the King's Schools Scheme, because some Trustees felt that charity doles encouraged laziness and dependency. In fact cynics might say that the King's Schools Scheme was only set up so that King Henry VIII's Charity could lay hands on other charity funds, so that it did not have to fund the modernisation alone.

Undoubtedly too much money intended for other purposes was sucked into the King's Schools Scheme, but in the 1870s many sincere people who were Trustees of the various charities thought that they were doing the right thing. It is easy for us to criticise, but one of the most unfortunate mistakes proved to be that most of the town charities, including that of King Henry VIII, sold off property following advice from the Charity Commissioners, converting the proceeds into Consols (Government Securities paying a good rate of interest).

The Sale of Property in 1877

Permission was obtained from the Charity Commissioners to sell off 20 properties; the most valuable being a farm which was situated in the area now centred on All Saints Road. Lady Percy lived at nearby Guy's Cliffe House and the farm adjoined Guy's Cliffe Park.

The pleasantly situated farm house, garden, orchard together with outbuildings was sold with land measuring 66 acres and 3 roods. There was also timber which alone was valued at £122 7sh. 6d. The whole was sold to Mr Handley who was acting as agent for Lady Percy and the large price of £10,000 reflected the importance of the site.

Numbers 33 and 35 Jury Street (from 1912 the site of the "Porridge Pot" Restaurant) were sold as one lot for £650, the buyer being a Mr Collins from Birmingham. Number 33 was then occupied by George Jack, a decorator, and Number 35 by William Wills, a boot and shoe maker.

Perhaps one of the best known properties in the town at that time was the Griffin Inn, situated at the corner of the Market Square, close to the Market Hall. Next to the Griffin was a house and boot and shoe shop occupied by William Sleath and it was Mr Sleath who purchased the whole for £2,610. Today the corner site is occupied by a gentlemen's outfitters, whilst next door is a camera shop.

For me the most emotive lot was Lot 20 ... two strips of unenclosed land in Barford Meadow sold for £190. The buyer was an agent for Miss Ryland of Sherbourne, whose land adjoined that for sale and when I saw her name, memories of my paternal grandmother came flooding back. Ellen Needle (later Box) had been born in Sherbourne in 1866, her family occupying one of the new cottages built for the estate workers. Kindly Louisa Ryland had taken a great interest in my grandmother and I reflected that nothing enlivens history quite as much as personal involvement.

Although a few lots were withdrawn , most were sold and the large total of £23,235 was raised from the sale and invested in Consols.

Many Properties Sold 1877 to 1985

As the Borough Fund increased in value and importance, so the Charity of King Henry VIII gradually slid into a position of lesser importance in comparison with previous centuries

The pattern established in 1877 was continued with more and more properties sold off and the proceeds converted to Consols.

The clearest picture of transactions from 1877 to 1959 can be obtained from reference to pages 121 to 125 in "The Estate of King Henry VIII" ... the unpublished typescript by E.G. Tibbits, a copy of which can be found in Warwickshire County Record Office. Those readers who are interested in seeking more detailed information about precise properties could find the information quickly and easily from the schedules contained there and also find out which available maps are relevant to each property.

With the limited space at my disposal, all I can do is compile a list, mentioning some sales and properties which may be of interest.

1878 ... 14 acres of land on South side of Myton Road given to Governors of Warwick School as site for new school buildings.

1888 ... 2950 sq. yards fronting to Myton Road sold to Warwick School Governors for £200.

1893 ... Cottage and 847 sq. yards on West side of Village Street in Chaddesley Corbett sold to Chaddesley Corbett Endowed School for £75.

1901 ... Various houses, cottages and land in Chaddesley Corbett sold at auction. Proceeds of over £1,000 invested in Consols.

1929 ... Piece of Lammas land in St Nicholas' Meadow sold to Warwick Corporation for over £190. (Around 5 acres which included the site of the Swimming Baths)

1938 ... The Market Hall in the Square, then housing the Museum, given to County Council who agreed to undertake repairs etc.

1940 ... 4 cottages and gardens in Chaddesley Corbett sold for £280.

1948 ... 21 acres of Lammas land in St Mary's Parish Warwick sold to Warwick Corporation for over £1,316.

...15 acres of Glebe land in Budbrooke sold to War Department for £1,565.

1950 ... Land adjacent to Warwick School sold to Trustees of the Warwick School Memorial Endowment Fund for £1750.

1958 …10.93 acres with a 500 frontage to Myton Road sold as site for new R.C. Secondary School (Dormer School) for £3,280. Proceeds of sale used to purchase Cottage Farm Myton (over 20 acres for £2,500 from Lord Warwick) and over 3 acres at Sales Close Budbrooke (purchased for £130). Compensation had to be paid to the tenant of Brook Farm, Myton.

1983 … Land along Myton Road sold for housing (Saumur Way etc)

Other Charities and the Trustees

In September 1836 the Lord Chancellor appointed 21 Trustees to administer the Warwick Municipal Charities, including the Charity of King Henry VIII. All the charities included had previously been administered by the inner council of Warwick Corporation.

In the beginning the Charities of Sir Thomas White, Francis Lord Guildford, the Hon. John Smith, the Countess of Devonshire, Robert Heath, Alderman Whateley, Richard Edgeworth, Nicholas Eyffler, Thomas Oken and William Viner were all included. All these Charities were administered by the same 21 men plus the official Clerk and Receiver. Within a few years, Oken's Charity was being administered separately (it should not have been included with the others anyway) and in 1956 the Charity of Nicholas Eyffler was transferred to be administered alongside Oken's by the Trustees of that Charity, as historically it always had been.

Today the only other Charity administered alongside that of King Henry VIII is Sir Thomas White's … all the others mentioned above being either absorbed by the Charity of King Henry VIII or amalgamated into the King's Schools Foundation in 1875

Traditionally administered alongside that of King Henry VIII Sir Thomas White's Charity benefits any needy young persons, desiring to establish themselves in business in Warwick who can apply to this Charity for an interest free loan (Maximum about £5,000) for a period of 2-3 years. Since 1552 the estate of Sir Thomas White has been used to benefit the young inhabitants of 5 Midlands towns … Warwick, Coventry, Northampton, Nottingham and Leicester. Money was paid to Warwick every 5th year and from 1875 £360 of the income was paid into the King's Schools fund and from 1882 the whole income was paid into the same fund … if no suitable young persons applied for loans. The assets of the Charity of Sir Thomas White are composed entirely of investment shares and money on deposit so administration is simplified. Both the Charity of King Henry VIII and the Charity of Sir Thomas White benefit the Warwick Schools Foundation, and there have been many times in the past when Sir Thomas White's has contributed more to the schools. In 1875 £25,000 of accumulated deposit was transferred to the newly formed King's Schools Foundation which was more than the contribution from the Charity of King Henry VIII.

In practice few of the Warwick Charities now act alone … some have been amalgamated and other groups have joined together to fund a particular project.

Since 1978 King Henry VIII's Charity has given grants to various projects run by other charities, including those connected with almshouses, and in order to understand the full working of King Henry's, it is necessary to have knowledge of the various other Warwick Charities.

As to the actual people who act as Trustees ... over the years some of the most respected and influential businessmen have served. In the 19th century, 21 men were co-optative Trustees for life, but in the 20th century, some Trustees have been nominated by elected bodies.

In the late 19th century there were some well known names in the list. The name of Thomas Kendall (1837-1919) the famous cabinet maker of Chapel Street will be familiar to many. He was a very fine wood-carver and he completed the chimney piece in the Mayor's Parlour in the Court House, choir stalls in the Lord Leycester Hospital Chapel and the pulpit in St Mary's Church, amongst many other items.

Around 1900 well known Trustees included Michael Lakin (cement manufacturer), John Margetts (auctioneer), Charles Bolt Shaw (wine merchant), Stephen Stanton (Mayor for several years) and James Plucknett (cabinet maker).

Brabazon Campbell, a solicitor and partner in the firm Campbell, Brown and Ledbrook, was also a Trustee for many years and when Town Clerk in 1890 he had compiled an official report into the Charities of Warwick.

Thomas Kemp (1848 -1924)

The writer of perhaps my favourite local history book "History of Warwick and Its People" published in 1906 contributed a huge amount to the Charity of King Henry VIII and other aspects of life in Warwick.

Born in Warwick on 5th January 1848, Thomas Kemp was articled to the legal firm of R.C. Heath in 1865. After passing his law examinations, Thomas Kemp worked for some years in the same office before retiring so that he could take a more active part in public life. In 1880 he was elected to Warwick Town Council and he was Mayor from 1892-4 and again from 1905-7, including the important Pageant Year of 1906. A keen Sunday School teacher for 25 years, he played a prominent part in the formation of the Beauchamp Chapel Restoration Fund in the early 1920s.

Thomas Kemp was a Trustee of several Warwick Charities, his involvement as a Trustee of King Henry VIII's Charity lasting for over 30 years. For many years he gave talks about the history of Warwick and he spent years transcribing the Minute Books of the Corporation and the old documents which today make up many in the collection attributed to King Henry VIII's Charity. He had the time to transcribe and publish The Black Book and The Book of John Fisher and today many students of Warwick history are able to read the fascinating tales for themselves.

For those who wish to find out more about this most interesting man, in Warwickshire County Record Office in Warwick there is a photograph album which he compiled between 1896 and 1921. Photographs of his home at 10 Jury Street (now the premises of solicitors Campbell, Brown and Ledbrook) local views and

personal items including photographs of his family and pets all bring the compiler and Warwick history to life. Photographs of the terrier Spark "the Pageant Dog" who died on 24th October 1911 and Old Tim the long-haired cat who died on 18th March 1914 make history more personal and therefore more interesting.

I think that Warwick owes a great deal to Thomas Kemp and so does the Charity of King Henry VIII.

Edward George Tibbits

Apart from Oken himself, I can think of no other individual who merits inclusion in a history of the Charity of King Henry VIII, for not only did he write a detailed account of the Charity (also most of the others in Warwick) but he was a most influential Trustee for many years.

Being a member of a long established professional family in Warwick (many of the family were solicitors or doctors) George, as he was usually known, had been

PICTURED IN THE "WARWICK ADVERTISER" IN JUNE 1956, SOLICITOR AND HISTORIAN E.G. TIBBITS RIDES A ROVER SAFETY BICYCLE ONCE GIVEN TO HIS FATHER JOHN IN 1898. A true son of the town, George did more than any other person of his time to help preserve the historical buildings, documents and traditions of Warwick. He is pictured outside his solicitor's practice (Moore & Tibbits) in High Street. (CW)

instrumental in persuading public opinion in Warwick to save several old buildings including the Market Hall and the Lord Leycester Hospital. In the 1930s the Trustees of King Henry VIII's Charity wished to rid themselves of the Market Hall which was needing many repairs. There were some who wished to demolish it and widen the roads in the vicinity, but George and others battled successfully and finally the Charity gave the premises to the County Council. After the war, the premises of the Lord Leycester Hospital were in urgent need of extensive restoration and again some argued that the cost was too high and it would be better to demolish some parts and build afresh. Again George, then Clerk to the Governors of the Hospital, helped to rally support and gradually the critics were silenced.

Mr Charles Wiseman, a legal executive who worked with George for many years both at the family firm of Moore and Tibbits and elsewhere, recalled how in 1942 George joined the Military Police and as an official historian was one of the first to enter the infamous Belsen concentration camp. Like Thomas Kemp, E.G. Tibbits gave many talks on the history of Warwick and he was Mayor of Warwick several times including the important Coronation Year of 1953 when he visited the Mayor of Warwick in Rhode Island, U.S.A. and sent greetings. As Clerk of Oken's Charity he was instrumental in reintroducing Oken's Feast, the celebration of which had lapsed and recently I could not help smiling when his cousin Elizabeth Tibbits recalled,

"I think George often thought of himself as a latter day Oken."

Once in 1957 I had the good fortune to have an interview with George Tibbits and he helped me a great deal with research I was carrying out as part of a college project concerning Ann Johnson's charity. Rather gruff at first, he soon softened and gave me around two hours of his time, growing more and more enthusiastic as time went on.

Also interested in the preservation of steam trains, George was a prominent member of the Talyllyn Railway Preservation Society near Cader Idris in mid Wales, which was the first R.P. society in the world. He was a trustee of King Henry VIII's Charity for many years during the 1930s, 1940s and 1950s and he was sadly missed when he died suddenly in 1969, aged only 64.

Recent Times

Around 1950, prominent Trustees included Alderman Guy Nelson (after whom the Guy Nelson Hall at Warwick School was named), Arthur H.B. Bishop (Headmaster of Warwick School), David H. Brown (Civil engineer) and H.J. Ansell, the General Manager and Director of the Warwick Building Society.

In more recent times the well known dental surgeon in Warwick R.A. Cohen, P.W. Martin then Headmaster of Warwick School, Captain Lee then Master of the Lord Leycester Hospital, the historians Philip Styles and H.R. (Dick) Hosking, Dr Stephen Whittaker of Bridge End, and local G.P. and Coroner Dr Stephen Tibbits were all Trustees for many years.

Herbert Walden C.B.E.

With over 30 years of service, the longest serving of the present Trustees is Herbert Walden of Leek Wootton who for many years was a Director, General Manager and Secretary of the Heart of England Building Society.

Having been born in Warwick, he showed great financial aptitude and quickly rose in rank in the Warwick Building Society which he joined on leaving school. From 1983 to 1985 he had national recognition as chairman of the Building Societies Association. On his retirement from Heart of England in 1986 he was the first part time member to be appointed to the newly formed regulatory body for building societies, the Building Societies Commission.

A quiet, unassuming yet amazingly shrewd man, Herbert Walden has had many other contacts with the Charity of King Henry VIII over the years, not only as Trustee. From 1955 to 1963 he served on Warwick Borough Council and for 28 years was a Governor of Warwick School, the King's High School For Girls and Warwick Preparatory School, being Chairman of the Foundation from 1986-1990. Besides being a Trustee of King Henry VIII's Charity, Mr Walden has also served in a similar capacity for Oken's and other Charities and he continues to make his vast knowledge of public finance available to the body of the Municipal Charity Trustees and many other local organisations.

HERBERT WALDEN C.B.E. IS CURRENTLY THE LONGEST SERVING TRUSTEE OF KING HENRY VIII'S CHARITY. (HW)

THIS PHOTOGRAPH WAS TAKEN AT OKEN'S FEAST IN 1955 AND ALMOST ALL THOSE FEATURED HAD DIRECT CONNECTIONS WITH KING HENRY VIII'S CHARITY. From left to right they are Alfred Knibbs, master printer and Deputy Mayor; Rev. Joseph McCulloch, Vicar of St Mary's; George Tibbits, Mayor, holding a silver replica of Oken's chest which now belongs to Oken's Charity; David Lord Brooke, now the 8th Earl of Warwick; and Lord de Lisle. (CW)

The Current Trustees

At present the Charity is administered under the 1978 scheme which directs that "ten competent persons" shall form the body of Trustees. Some of the men and women who currently act as Trustees of the Municipal Charities, including that of King Henry VIII, have served for many years.

At the time of writing (1st September 1994) there are nine Trustees. The 4 nominated by various bodies are

1) Barry Gillitt D.L., M.A., F.C.A. (Chartered Accountant)... the nominee of the Bishop of Coventry

2) K.T. Meredith (Gentleman)... the nominee of the Archdeacon of Warwick

3) D.G. Fuller (Solicitor) ... the nominee of the Warwick Schools Foundation

4) Mrs M. Haywood (Company Director) ... the nominee of Warwick Town Council

The other Trustees are co-optative, that is to say they are invited in the first instance by the other Trustees, often to supply a certain expertise, e.g. financial or legal. These names appear in alphabetical order.

5) B. Brewster (Company Director and currently Mayor of Warwick)

6) J.P. McCarthy (Solicitor, former Town Councillor and Warwick resident)

7) Mrs S.M. Rhodes (Garden Historian)

8) N.F. J. Thurley (Chartered Quantity Surveyor)

9) H.R.C. Walden C.B.E. (Building Societies Commissioner)

All the Trustees serve for a set period, the Nominative Trustees for 4 years and the Co-optative Trustees for 3 or 5 years, unless for illness or some other reason they retire before their term is finished.

The Trustees cannot take any course of action outside the scope of their approved Scheme. Should they wish to do so, they must first resolve the matter themselves and then seek the approval of the Charity Commission to formally amend the scheme. This was done in 1987 when the Trustees resolved that the church share of their income should be distributed in a different manner and other parishes included. The revision was negotiated with and approved by the Charity Commissioners.

In the old days it was the Court of Chancery who made decisions as to how the Estate was to be administered and how much was to be paid out in salaries, but the Charity Commission was set up in the mid 19th century and it is still the regulatory body. There are firm rules as to how charities are run, as for instance the rule that the money from land sales must be re-invested in property and any profit from such sales is re-invested as part of the Permanent Endowment of the Charity and not treated as income.

Obviously any charity is only as good as its Trustees, for wrong decisions made by ignorant people can have a disastrous effect on long term prosperity. In many ways a mixture of elected representatives and co-optative Trustees works well for those with particular expertise in some field can often be persuaded to serve, although they might not seek election on a local council for instance, because of the bureaucracy and time spent in meetings.

I am not a Trustee of any charity, but since researching my first book which concerned Ann Johnson's Charity in Warwick, I have come to realise how important charities were in the past, are at present and will be in the future.

The Trustees are not paid for their services, although the Clerk obviously has considerable administrative expenses which are paid from income, subject to the scrutiny of Auditors and the Charity Commission. Why then do the Trustees bother if they are unpaid? I believe the answer lies in the fact they have enormous satisfaction in seeing a job well done for the benefit of all. Trustees earn themselves a niche in history, for it is an honour to be invited to serve.

MANY OF THE PEOPLE ON THIS HISTORIC PHOTOGRAPH OF WARWICK TOWN COUNCIL IN APRIL 1956 WERE TRUSTEES OF KING HENRY VIII'S CHARITY. From left to right they are (Back row) Frank Walker (Mace Bearer), Henry Thistleton (Beadle), Fred Blakemore (Mace Bearer). (3rd row)...Jim Wallsgrove, Frank Walters, Victor Robinson, Denis Grimes, Henry Lewis, Ted Bartlett, Peter Hinchcliffe. (2nd row)... Dr H. Stephen Tibbits, Dr Stephen Whittaker, Fred Vittle, Bill Mountford, Bill Tarver, Eric Lloyd Averns, Iris Lees, Tenneson Lees, Lionel Hodges, Jim McGrouther, Herbert Walden. (Front row) V. Collier, Herbert Ansell, Guy Nelson, Humphrey Dolphin (Town Clerk), George Tibbits (Mayor), Rev. Dr Frankland (Mayor's Chaplain), Alfred Knibbs, Charles Holmes, Thomas Bromwich. This was the first time the Town Council had been photographed in their robes and the first meeting in the Lord Leycester Hospital since the time of Thomas Oken. (Reproduced by permission of Warwickshire County Record Office)

The Clerks of the Charity

The role of Clerk and Receiver of Rents for the Charity has always been an important one and as in any other business, a resourceful and skillful Clerk has made a huge difference to the management of affairs.

After 1769 when Warwick Corporation had control of King Henry VIII's Charity restored to it, Thomas Greenway was the nominated official Receiver of Rents and Profits and following his death in 1804, the office was offered to Kelynge Greenway.

In the later nineteenth century Richard Child Heath was an important figure and he was clerk to several important Charities including King Henry VIII's and the King's Schools.

Born in 1833 and educated at Warwick School under Rev. Herbert Hill, Richard Child Heath was the son of Thomas Heath, a previous Town Clerk of Warwick and well known local lawyer. However both father and son had numerous connections with the Liberal Party and as such were not selected by the largely Tory Town Council for some prestigious appointments.

It would seem that the complicated details of the King's Schools Scheme owed much to the diligence of R.C. Heath who loved his native town and was determined to help place Warwick School on a sure footing. Exceptionally hard working until his death in 1913, he was universally respected in the Warwick area.

Henry Maxwell Blenkinsop (the grandson of the wife of R.C. Heath) was Clerk from 1913 to his death in 1968 and his son Gerald carried on the family tradition until his retirement in 1983.

When I visited Gerald Blenkinsop at his home in Warwick in late 1993 he told me of his family's involvement with King Henry VIII's Charity.

"I enjoyed visiting the Ilmington property in particular" he recalled and I replied that I could well understand that.

With charities, as with other businesses, circumstances change and chartered surveyor Peter Butler has been Clerk and Receiver of Rents since 1983. Previously called in as a property consultant, his appointment has made very good sense in a period when several major land deals have been negotiated by the Charity.

PROPERTY AND ASSETS

From pre Norman times, the owners of Warwick Castle were the largest property owners in the locality, but from 1545 King Henry VIII's Charity became a most important land owner in Warwick.

Originally being endowed with property and privileges which had once belonged to St Mary's Collegiate Church, the Charity was given other land by the Guild of Warwick and later other properties were bought as investments or given by individuals. Unlike some other charities, from the onset, King Henry VIII's Charity was based on land ownership, which together with tithes, meant a steady income from the rents.

At some time or another in the past four and a half centuries many of the important buildings in Warwick, (except the Castle, Priory and St John's House) have been owned by King Henry VIII's Charity. Most of the older properties have long since been sold off or transferred, but a few of the original properties still remain in the list of those owned today.

PROPERTY AND CHURCH PRIVILEGES ORIGINALLY GRANTED TO ST MARY'S

l) Tithes

It is often difficult to understand the importance of religion in the lives of our forebears. Not only did the year begin on Lady Day, 25th March (as a mark of respect for the Virgin Mary) until the 18th century, but also rectors (and vicars to a lesser degree) of English parish churches were entitled to tithes (one tenth of crops) from within the parish. The tithe system had been established in Saxon times, possibly as early as the 7th century and the income of many Parsons relied heavily on such payments in kind.

At the Reformation, when King Henry VIII abolished many religious establishments, many tithe rights passed to the Crown, but in the case of Warwick, these tithe entitlements were given to the town as part of the Estate of King Henry VIII.

Without going into complicated details, King Henry VIII's Charity enjoyed substantial tithe rights in the four parishes in which the Corporation acted as the Rector. The parishes were St Mary's and St Nicholas' in Warwick, Budbrooke and also Chaddesley Corbett. Early account books of the Charity include details of the *"privy tithes and offerings, and other premises belonging to the church and parish of St*

Mary in Warwick" ... tithes of corn and hay in fields of Longbridge; tithes of lamb and wool in Longbridge and St Lawrence; tithes of herbage of the Lee Fields in the marshes of Combwell; of the enclosed grounds, parcel of Wedgnock Park, then disparked; of the common ground within Wedgnock Park then imparked, and within the parish of St Mary; the rent of St Mary's church-yard and charnel-house; the rents of the tithe ... pig, geese, eggs, fruit and garden tithe within the said parish; rent of the tithe-barn and close; the privy tithes offerings and dues on marriages, christenings and burials.

It was a similar situation in the other parishes controlled by the Corporation of Warwick.

However the tithes were not only to benefit the parson; a portion also had to be given to the Bishop, with some used for the benefit of the church fabric and the poor. In 1571 in the Black Book John Fisher mentioned that as a result of the Tithes and First Fruits, the Bishop of Worcester was paid £1.0.0 annually and the Archdeacon of Worcester 16sh 8d. All the four parishes were then in the Diocese of Worcester as the Diocese of Coventry was not instituted until the 20th century.

The subject of tithes is generally complicated as there were local variations, but basically the story was the same. Sometimes payment was not enforced or people could not afford to give, but on the whole it seems that tithes became a habit and throughout the centuries, a somewhat grudging payment was made to ensure a quiet life. Some groups of people did refuse to pay, the Quakers for example and this was perhaps an additional reason why many Quakers were imprisoned in Warwick in 1661 in the dreadful octagonal dungeon under the Shire Hall. (This can still be viewed at certain times... complete with hole for the cesspit and frogs!)

There are numerous examples of tithes being leased out by the Corporation of Warwick and as with property they were leased out for lengthy periods.

Some idea of the value of these tithes can be had from lists of the Charity's assets in the early 19th century, compiled by E.G. Tibbits. Altogether King Henry VIII's Charity owned 480 acres of land including 280 acres in the vicinity of Warwick, 108 acres (plus buildings) in Budbrooke, 39 acres and a house at Ilmington and 40 acres and houses at Chaddesley Corbett.

The total income from the property was £2,761 14sh 9d yet the income from tithes alone in the Warwick and Budbrooke area was £758. The lucrative tithes of Chaddesley were included in the £740 paid annually by Sir Charles Throckmorton who leased 37 acres of the land there and including this sum, the total amount of money raised by tithes was £237 greater than the amount raised by property.

Apples, Eggs, Corn, Hay and Other Tithes Phased Out

Some tithes disappeared when the fields were enclosed in the 18th and 19th centuries and the payment of tithes in kind was abolished by the Tithes Commutation Act of 1836. Many people had felt for a long time that the church being entitled to a tenth of a crop, apples for instance, was a totally outdated idea and there was no doubt that there had been many abuses of the system.

After 1836 tithes were replaced by a Tithe rent charge and often a one-off payment redeemed the obligation. For example some tithes in Budbrooke on fields with the glorious sounding names of Sow Meadow and Further Boggy Meadow had been redeemed in 1878 for payments of £42 and £74 respectively.

In the case of King Henry VIII's Charity, much of the land had already been sold off by the 20th century but some small rent charges continued until the mid 20th century. Around 1960 a small rent charge was still being paid by the Smith Ryland Estate in respect of a tithe dole in the Lower Norton Town Fields in Budbrooke.

"Alas, Poor Yoric!"

In past centuries it did not seem to bother anyone that human bones were frequently being dug up and whereas we are squeamish about such matters today, with all bodies being buried (cremation was not legal in England until 1885) many churchyards had to be used over and over again. The charnel house was the crypt or bone house and it gives us a strong reminder of Shakespeare's "Hamlet". The crypt at St Mary's was used for piling the human bones which from time to time were dug up from the churchyard and during the reign of Elizabeth I there were records of the crypt being leased for 21 years. One man usually had the job of picking up the bones and when St Mary's was being rebuilt in 1697, there were so many bones disturbed that a special collecting basket was provided.

Some readers might be surprised that the church-yard could be leased. The answer was that in the days before lawnmowers animals would graze in the churchyard and it was these grazing rights which were leased.

We often seem to forget that until the 20th century, death was very much a fact of life and far more people died in infancy or when young than lived to grow old. So all the population were very familiar with funerals, churchyards, coffins and bones.

2) Buildings and Land

For centuries St Mary's had owned houses and land in or around Warwick and these properties were granted to King Henry VIII's Estate. The Deanery of St Mary's, the Rectory of St Nicholas and houses in Warwick were all included and there was also property in Budbrooke.

However perhaps the most interesting and one of the most lucrative parts of the church property was that in Worcestershire at Chaddesley Corbett.

Chaddesley Corbett

In the late fourteenth century, when the last member of the Corbett family died, much of the land in the village of Chaddesley Corbett passed to the Beauchamp family in Warwick. Thomas Beauchamp the younger, Earl of Warwick from 1370-97 and 1399-1401 gave a large portion of the manor of Chaddesley Corbett to the Collegiate Church of St Mary in Warwick to pay for the new church then under construction. In 1394 , the advowson of Chaddesley Corbett Church was given to

THIS IS ONE OF THE PHOTOGRAPHS OF THE MAIN STREET OF CHADDESLEY CORBETT, IN WORCESTERSHIRE, TAKEN IN JULY OR AUGUST 1892 AND INCLUDED IN THE COLLECTION OF ALDERMAN THOMAS KEMP OF WARWICK. From 1545 onwards King Henry VIII's Charity owned many of the properties in the main village street, but many were sold at auction in 1901. (Reproduced by permission of Warwickshire County Records Office)

St Mary's which retained the right to appoint the vicar until 1544 when St Mary's voluntarily gave up all its possessions.

In 1545, by the Deed setting up the Charity of King Henry VIII, numerous properties in the Worcestershire village and also the advowson of the church were granted back to the town of Warwick. From 1545 to 1639, the right to appoint the vicar of Chaddesley Corbett, also the vicars of the nearby parishes of Rushock and Stone, was vested in the Corporation. After a row between Warwick Corporation and the Crown, in 1637 Warwick Corporation lost the right to the advowson in the three parishes and since that time, the Crown has appointed the vicars. However King Henry VIII's Charity still remained as the Corporate Lay Rector of the parish and as such was entitled to the lucrative tithes.

Those who know the village, which is situated about 5 miles from Bromsgrove, will know how attractive it is and that is why in 1969 Chaddesley Corbett was designated as one of the first Conservation Areas in the country. Most older properties in the village are listed Grade II (group value) and St Cassian's Church has a Grade I listing. In the course of four and a half centuries, most of the properties in the village once owned by the Charity have been sold and today the Trustees control just two important buildings in the village ... Bluntington Farm and The Swan Inn.

"ELIZABETH COTTAGE" IN CHADDESLEY CORBETT AS IT WAS IN 1974. In 1974 the Trustees of King Henry VIII's Charity applied for permission to demolish these old cottages and build another house on the site. Planning permission was refused so the building was sold and alterations and extensions were carried out in 1976 by the new owner. Today the attractive dwelling, whilst still retaining much of the original timber frame, bears little resemblance to the picturesque, but near derelict building in this photograph. (Reproduced by permission of Warwickshire County Record Office)

A Map of Chaddesley Corbett by James Fish in 1697.

To my mind by far the most beautiful document belonging to the collection concerning the Charity of King Henry VIII is the map of *"Part of the Manour of Chadsley Corbett in the county of Worcester, being the Lands belonging to the Corporation of Warwick."*

When researching my previous book concerning Landor House in Warwick, through examining various surveys and documents he had written as Chief Trustee of Ann Johnson's Charity, I came to respect the meticulous Warwick surveyor with his distinctive, neat handwriting. I was delighted to find his 1697 survey listed amongst the charity documents and I spent a happy hour enjoying the small, but artistic map which was to a scale of one inch to 132 feet.

In 1697 almost all the houses in the village belonged to the Corporation of

Warwick. The Charity's possessions were neatly labelled and outlined in yellow and I was fascinated as I admired the technical skill of James Fish. Born in 1673, he was the son of the James Fish the elder, Parish Clerk of St Mary's and father and son had numerous connections with St Mary's.

Bluntington Farm

On the edge of Chaddesley Corbett, on the Drayton Road, stands an extremely picturesque, half-timbered property known as Bluntington Farm. Having been constructed in the 17th century, the house had alterations and additions in the 19th and 20th centuries. This grade II listed building has the date 1680 and WK (an abbreviation for Warwick Corporation?) high on a prominent gable and interesting outbuildings and magnificent garden add to the charm of the property.

When I first visited the property in the summer of 1993, tenant William Beveridge explained, *"You can see the people on the Malvern Hills from here on a clear day"* and I grew quite envious of the farm and open situation. Mr Beveridge and his family have leased the property for many years and I found the fact that he had 52 acres (33 of them rented from the Charity) planted with rhubarb very interesting.

BLUNTINGTON FARM ON THE OUTSKIRTS OF CHADDESLEY CORBETT HAS BELONGED TO KING HENRY VIII'S CHARITY FOR CENTURIES. The half timbered house with its oak beams and inglenook fireplaces is full of character and high on a gable are the letters WK (for Warwick?) 1680. (JF)

On my second visit, Ben, the resident Staffordshire Bull Terrier, gave me his fullest attention as I chatted to Mrs Beveridge about the history of the farm. On the 1697 map there was a garden in a similar position to that shown today, with a yard and an orchard adjoining the farmhouse, which was opposite to Bluntington Green. Behind the orchard, an area labelled hemp butts occupied just over a quarter of an acre.

The Swan Inn

As with Bluntington Farm, it would appear that the Charity has owned the site of the Swan Inn since 1545. On the map of 1697 the site of the Swan and its car parks was occupied by tenements rented by Widow Hunt. There were two large bays of a brick building with a thatched roof, together with stables and various barns. In the 18th century the property was made into one, with part being used as an Inn.

Today The Swan is a flourishing establishment, with the old stable block being converted into a comfortable lounge bar, where a variety of bar-meals can be

THE SITE OF THE SWAN INN AT CHADDESLEY CORBETT HAS PROBABLY BELONGED TO KING HENRY VIII'S CHARITY SINCE 1545. First referred to as an inn in the 18th century, the present building seems to date largely from the 19th century. Leased by Batham's Brewery, Brierley Hill, the inn has several bars, a restaurant and a large garden. Like the best of traditional country inns, the Swan has odd corners, convenient hatches and hand-pulled draught beer so it is no wonder it seems popular with local people and visitors alike. (JF)

enjoyed. On my first visit in June 1993, my salad and jacket potato tasted all the better for my being able to admire the view across the garden to the open fields where sheep grazed contentedly. There was also a restaurant where delicious full meals were being served, but alas I was in a hurry.

The Brierley Brewery D. Batham and Sons have leased the inn for several decades and apart from the usual wines and spirits, traditional hand-pulled draught beer is still served. On my first visit, in the bar, Dennis Pardoe, Roy Evans, Gwyn Davis and other locals patiently answered my historical queries before entertaining me with tales of the village in the days of their boy-hood. The Swan Inn seemed deservedly popular and I congratulated tenant Keith Wales on maintaining a traditional yet lively atmosphere.

PROPERTY WHICH ORIGINATED FROM THE GUILD OF WARWICK

In addition to the Estate given by King Henry VIII the Guild of Warwick transferred some of its assets to the control of the new Corporation. The Guild itself was abolished in 1548, but because Thomas Oken and the other far-sighted leaders of the Guild had already obtained a charter legally setting up a town corporation (headed by themselves) it was possible to save the property for the town. For the first few years, accounts for the Guild Estate were listed separately because it seemed as if thinking people (Oken?) in those times left nothing to chance. They were constantly worried that the Crown might confiscate some or all of the town's possessions. The mid 16th century was a particularly volatile period with many plots and executions for political and religious reasons.

Over the 450 years most properties have been sold, but there is one piece of Guild land still in the possession of King Henry VIII's Charity.

The Guild property which was transferred in 1545 was –

1) Warwick … 5 tenements in High Pavement, opposite the Lord Leycester Hospital (one with a meadow); one tenement in Jury Street; one tenement and two cottages in St Nicholas Street; one tenement in the Market Place; one tenement in West Street and land in Coten Field. Also there was the Guildhall itself and other property which now forms part of the Lord Leycester Hospital.

2) Elsewhere … a tenement in Henley, land in Hatton, a house and land in Ilmington; a house and garden in Radford and land in Woodcote, Norton and Snitterfield (later Beausale).

Ilmington

For the 450 years of its existence, the Charity of King Henry VIII has owned property in the parish of Ilmington over twenty miles from Warwick, in the extreme south of Warwickshire. When I visited the Charity land in Ilmington on a bright April morning in 1994, I left the car on a verge beside the narrow road to

THESE HOUSES IN HIGH STREET (FORMERLY CALLED HIGH PAVEMENT)
WERE ONCE OWNED BY THE GUILD OF WARWICK, AS WERE HOUSES
ADJOINING THE HOSPITAL ON THE OPPOSITE SIDE OF THE ROAD. The fact
that they all survived the Great Fire in 1694 and today form a wonderful group around
Westgate much adds to the atmosphere, for these houses are still visible from the windows of
the former Guildhall, much as they were in the 16th century. (JF)

Charingworth, to the south of the village of Ilmington. The call of the cuckoo in a
nearby wood was the only distinguishable sound, apart from a farm tractor in the
far distance and the chilly wind was sufficient to rustle the new leaves in the hedge
at the side of the ancient bridle path.

I walked along the ancient track known as Pig Lane knowing the land on either
side was once owned by "The Trustees of the Warwick Poor" as the Charity was
often referred to on maps in the nineteenth century. Today 31 acres of the land
between Pig Lane and Ilmington is still owned by the Charity and although there
are no buildings, this pasture land must rank as being one of the most historical and
attractive Charity assets of all.

The Guild of Warwick Owned Land

Quite why in the sixteenth century the ancient Guild of Warwick owned land in
the picturesque village of Ilmington is not clear. Perhaps the land at the
southernmost extremity of Warwickshire provided a good investment because it
contained excellent land for grazing sheep, before they were despatched to the
nearby sheep market of Shipston On Stour, which at that time was one of the most
important in England.

THE FORMER GUILDHALL IN THE LORD LEYCESTER HOSPITAL IS CERTAINLY A PLACE TO STIR THE IMAGINATION. In this room from 1545 till 1571, Thomas Oken and the other Burgesses of the town discussed how to administer the Estate of King Henry VIII. I never tire of visiting this interesting room which was built around 1450 by Neville "The Kingmaker" Earl of Warwick. (JF)

THE GREAT HALL OF KING JAMES IN THE LORD LEYCESTER HOSPITAL. Erected around 1383, it was used by the Warwick Guild and later until 1571 by the Corporation as a banqueting hall and schoolroom. In 1617 Sir Fulke Greville and the Corporation entertained King James I here, hence the name, but the expenses incurred bankrupted the town for several years. Today the refurbished hall is a popular venue for a variety of meetings, including appropriately Oken's Annual Feast. (JF)

At any rate the Warwick Guild owned various pieces of (unenclosed) land and a farm in Ilmington. In 1544 John Jenkes, the Master, and the Brethren of the Guild in Warwick leased the farm house and outbuildings, together with 34 acres of arable, meadow and pasture land called Noland, The Hill, The Dairy Ground, The Meadow and Wedgenock to Richard Petty of Ilmington in 1544. The lease was surrendered by the Guild to the Bailiff and Burgesses of Warwick when all the Guild property was transferred to the Charity of King Henry VIII.

In 1808 Francis Canning of Foxcote House exchanged several pieces of land with the Charity Trustees. Land closer to the village of Ilmington was exchanged for land on Knowl Hill which adjoined the somewhat isolated Foxcote House.

A Sad Story?

Occasionally some seemingly rather dull documents are found to contain a poignant human story and so it was concerning the lease of Park Farm, Ilmington in 1777.

On 4th February 1777 the Corporation of Warwick as Trustees of the Charity had to apply to the Justices of the Peace because of the problem with Park Farm. For a whole year the rent had not been paid and it appeared that the tenant Francis Ganderton "*had deserted the premises and had left the same uncultivated and unoccupied*". After investigation the complaint was found to be true, but quite what had happened to Francis Ganderton was not made clear. Had he been unable to pay the rent and done a "moonlight flit" or had something more sinister happened? I did not find the answer to the mystery.

The problem with the lease was solved by the publishing of notices as to the reletting of the property.

> "*Notice is hereby given that a messuage or tenement and yard with the appurtenances situate at Ilmington in the County of Warwick and in the occupation of Francis Ganderton will be let to the Best Bidder on the seventeenth day of March next at the Shire Hall within the Borough of Warwick between the hours of ten and two of the clock on the same day. Dated the ninth day of February 1777*" By order of the Corporation of the said Borough.

Today the resale of repossessed property is advertised in local newspapers, but in the eighteenth century, it was up to the Parish Clerk to read out the notice after the services. It would appear that the notice about the property in Ilmington was read out in St Mary's Church Warwick as well as in St Mary's Ilmington … church services being perhaps the most reliable way of reaching a population, most of whom could not read.

Springs Supply the Village with Water

The Charity land at Ilmington included a spring which was the source of the local water supply for much of the twentieth century. Wedgnock Spring, not far from the footpath from Crab Mill Lane, was supplying about 8,000 gallons a day in 1928, the water running into a tank before being piped the short distance to the village.

Amongst the documents connected with the Charity are leases to Shipston on Stour Rural District Council, the lease in 1937 being accompanied by an interesting map indicating a proposed new collecting chamber for a spring known as Charity Spring which was slightly higher up the hill than Wedgnock Spring. In 1937 Shipston On Stour R.D.C. agreed the annual water rent of £10 with a wayleave rent of 10 shillings.

In 1941 Shipston on Stour R.D.C. agreed an annual water rent of £15 with a wayleave rent of £1.10sh for water from the Wedgnock Spring and Charity Spring. A new reservoir of reinforced concrete to hold 12,000 gallons was to be built, buried in the ground and all but the inspection cover to be covered with soil. This arrangement continued until around 1960 when alterations in council and water board responsibilities, coupled with increased demand, meant that other arrangements were made for the water supply of the village.

However I am assured by a recently retired employee of Severn Trent Water that the two springs, old pipeline and reservoir still remain hidden in a lush meadow in the charity land in Ilmington. Which just goes to prove that even the water supply of a village has an interesting history.

An Unchanging Landscape?

When I paid yet another visit to the Charity land at Ilmington, in the spring of 1994, I looked across the fields to Foxcote House and mused what a delightful, unspoilt part of Warwickshire this was. Apart from the hedges, this land close to Ilmington Downs has probably changed little in centuries and it is easy to develop a sense of history whilst gazing at the beautiful scenery.

Even today certain areas near to Ilmington are remote and steeped in folk lore and several emotive places lie close to the Charity land. The village of Hidcote Bartrim is only two or three miles away on foot up Pig Lane with the National Trust Gardens at Hidcote Manor being a little further on. Historic Compton Scorpion Manor, the home of Sir Thomas Overbury who was sensationally murdered in the Tower of London in 1613 is three miles distant, again most easily reached via Pig Lane. Legendary Meon Hill, topped by an Iron Age fort, was the site of the macabre "witchcraft murder" 50 years ago and it is only five miles away on foot. On St Valentine's Day 1945, farm labourer Charles Walton was found dead on Meon Hill his body pinned to the ground by his own pitchfork; his face grotesquely twisted with terror. The murderer could easily have walked away unnoticed down Pig Lane.

The narrow road to Charingworth is seldom busy and to wander on foot along ancient Pig Lane, past the Charity land, is to step into a timeless scene, where tales of ghosts abound, little changed since the pack horses of wealthy merchants such as Thomas Oken splashed through the mud. Although Park Farm was sold some years ago, King Henry VIII's Charity still owns 31 acres of pasture land, in much the same area as did the Guild of Warwick well over 450 years ago.

A TRADITIONAL WOODEN STILE LEADS INVITINGLY TO A FOOTPATH CROSSING SOME OF THE CHARITY'S LAND AT ILMINGTON. Originally owned by the Guild of Warwick, the Ilmington property has remained in the possession of King Henry VIII's Charity for 450 years. (JF)

PUBLIC BUILDINGS IN WARWICK DIRECTLY ASSOCIATED WITH THE CHARITY

1) The Lord Leycester Hospital

This most historic and picturesque half-timbered building was directly connected with King Henry VIII's Estate and the Corporation from 1545 to 1571, but there were many other associations both before and since.

In 1383 the newly formed Guild of St George the Martyr was granted the Chantry Chapel above Westgate and the room now known as The Great Hall of St James was built, probably by money given by Thomas Beauchamp, Earl of Warwick from 1370-97 and 1399 -1401. Between 1392 and 1415 the Guild of St George was amalgamated with the Guild of Holy Trinity and St Mary, thus forming a United Guild of Warwick which used the room as a meeting place and function room.

For some years in the mid 16th century, the King's Grammar School (Warwick School) used this room during the day and when King James I visited Warwick in 1617, Sir Fulke Greville was unable to entertain the King at Warwick Castle which was being re-built, so this room was used instead hence the name.

The upper room known as the Guildhall on the eastern side of the site was built around 1450 by Neville, Earl of Warwick usually known as "The Kingmaker". This was the Private Council Chamber of the United Guild of Warwick and in 1545 when the Council of the Guild, led by Thomas Oken, secured the town's first charter, the early Corporation meetings (inner council members only) were held there.

In 1571 Robert Dudley, the powerful Earl of Leycester, was granted the group of buildings so that he could found the hospital for old soldiers which still bears his name. So the school and the Corporation had to find alternative accommodation and 6 years after they were promised, the town was granted Eastgate (St Peter's Chapel), the Shire Hall and the Cross Tavern, which stood on the site of the present Court House. By that time the chantry chapels above both Eastgate and Westgate had fallen into disuse after the Reformation and the Earls of Leycester and Warwick granted the town some money for repairs because there was insufficient income from King Henry VIII's Estate to pay.

From 1571 the buildings were cared for by the endowment of the Earl of Leycester. Alterations took place in the 18th century, especially to the Master's house and a drastic restoration of St James Chapel and other parts was completed in the 1850s. A century later, the old buildings were in a terrible state of repair and extensive restoration was carried out from 1958-1966, thanks largely to the influence of E.G. Tibbits who as Clerk to the Governors of the Hospital persuaded the majority that the unique medieval buildings ought to be restored as near as possible to their original appearance.

In recent times there have been many links between the buildings and the Charity. As Charity profits increased during the 1980s, so more money was available for town use and several substantial grants have assisted repairs to the Guildhall Roof and the town wall. The present Master is Captain Dermot Rhodes and he has constant maintainance problems with such an ancient property.

The garden adjoining the buildings is at present undergoing restoration and I reflected how fitting it was that money from the Charity should be used for this purpose in 1994. One of the Charity's documents dated 22nd May 1565 allowed Thomas Sheldon to lease the doves and dovehouse, situated in the orchard or garden commonly called the Guildhall Garden. Exactly 430 years later the same garden (and dovehouse now adapted into a gazebo?) is being aided by money flowing in the opposite direction.

The Booth Hall

The 14th century Booth Hall stood in the Market Place to the north of the present Museum (Market Hall) and it was granted to the Corporation in the Charter of 1554. Of the 50 or so market stalls, some inside the hall and some round the walls outside, most were let to butchers. A glance through the numerous leases paints a colourful picture of shopping in the 16th and 17th centuries where tailors, ironmongers, barbers, glovers, whittawers (workers of white leather) and hosiers all plied their trade, alongside butchers, some of whom rented shambles (slaughtering areas) inside the hall. The rents of the Booth Hall were supposed to form part of a separate account known as the Bailiff's Account, to supplement the proceeds of King Henry VIII's Estate by funding such items as civic entertaining. However in practice the Bailiff's Account was not kept separate.

Around 1791, the Hall which had become dilapidated was demolished and sadly no drawings exist of this ancient structure.

The Shire Hall

The Shire Hall (originally known as the Steward's Place) was one of a group of buildings granted to the Corporation in 1576 by the Earls of Warwick and Leycester. Having been rebuilt or repaired in 1576, the property was given to the Corporation on condition the Judges and Sheriff could continue their sessions there. After the loss of the Guildhall in 1571 the Corporation used the Shire Hall whenever a large hall was needed and the election of the Bailiff took place there in 1573, 1574 and 1581.

When Ambrose Dudley, Earl of Warwick died in 1590 the Shire Hall was taken back by the Crown, but in 1595 it was leased to the Corporation who eventually bought back the freehold. It continued to be used for the Assizes and Quarter Sessions and there was also a House of Correction and a gaol.

By 1676 the County was responsible for the Shire Hall and all connections with the Corporation and the Charity of King Henry VIII ceased. It was rebuilt by William Hurlbutt soon afterwards and further rebuilding took place in 1753 -8, the present Judges House being built in 1814. Today the large Shire Hall complex, extended in 1966, houses County Council Offices besides a Crown Court where serious cases are still tried.

I cannot think of the Shire Hall without reflecting that over the centuries thousands of people must have received sentence of death there, before they were taken to the nearby gallows to be hanged. In the early days the gallows was at Gallows Hill on the Heathcote Lane, but later public executions took place on a site now occupied by part of Barrack Street, indeed 3 iron rings can still be seen (2 on the Shire Hall side and 1 in the wall of the Methodist Church Hall) which held the ropes which kept back the crowd on such occasions.

On a happier note, a document of 1674 connected with the Charity of King Henry VIII leased the garden of the Shire Hall to Robert Charnocke for 5 shillings. Over 320 years later there is still a small patch of private garden at the Shire Hall, complete with attractive trellis, lawn and tubs of flowering plants.

Eastgate

In the reign of Henry VI, probably around 1426, a Chapel to St Peter had been built above Eastgate to replace an earlier St Peter's Church in High Street. Like St James' Chapel over Westgate, St Peter's was a chantry chapel maintained by the

Guild of Warwick and a priest sang the traditional masses for the souls of the dead. Following the English Reformation and the abolition of the Guilds in 1548, St Peter's like St James' Chapel was unused and in bad condition and in 1576 money was provided by the Earls of Warwick and Leycester for repairs as there was insufficient spare income from King Henry VIII's Estate to pay for major expenditure. From 1577 it is believed that the Grammar School moved in and remained there for a number of years (until 1590?) when the school moved to a disused church in the Market Place and St Peter's Chapel was let as living accommodation.

As with other properties, in 1590 Eastgate was declared to be Crown property but eventually the Corporation bought back the freehold and for much of the 17th century St Peter's Chapel was leased as a family home.

In 1700 St Peter's was adapted as a schoolroom with accommodation built above for the master. To start with Oken's will provided £2 towards the salary, but in 1719 Sarah Greville's Charity (later several others) enlarged the school and the Bablake Charity School as it became known was firmly established. This school provided excellent education for needy youngsters for around 150 years and several times the accommodation for scholars had to be enlarged.

For much of the 19th century the schoolmaster was Samuel Gazey, like several Bablake School schoolmasters, an ex-pupil himself. Strict, but well liked, Samuel Gazey and his wife and family lived in the upper rooms of St Peter's Chapel, which, together with the gateway had been rebuilt (recased in stone) in 1788 by Francis Hiorne of Warwick. In 1841 not only were Samuel and Ann Gazey and their four children living in St Peter's Chapel, but so were an assistant teacher, and a servant girl. By day there were 120 pupils on the cramped site.

The clock on Eastgate had been provided by the will of Fulke Weale who died in 1729 and the schoolmaster was often paid extra to wind it weekly ... Samuel Gazey was paid 10sh 6d each year.

In 1875 the Bablake School was closed and the charity funds diverted into the King's Schools Foundation, so St Peter's Chapel once more became a house. In 1916 the nearby King's High School rented the property and they still rent it today.

In 1983 King Henry VIII's Charity sold the building to Mr J. Adcock, a chartered accountant living in Lapworth. However as the Charity still maintain the clock, Sidney Miles the present caretaker of the King's High School continues the long tradition of clock winding. He told me recently that it is one of his favourite weekly tasks, despite the fact that it necessitates an arduous climb up vertical ladders.

The Court House

Pevsner refers to this building as "Warwick at its best" and I feel sure the builder-architect Francis Smith of Warwick would have been flattered to think that 270 years on, his creation would have been thus appreciated. Also perhaps the Corporation of 1724 who ordered the new building to replace the older, somewhat dilapidated civic premises, ought to be congratulated, for at the time they were criticised and a serious official complaint was made.

THIS PAINTING OF EASTGATE AND ST PETER'S CHAPEL REALLY SEEMS TO CAPTURE THE SPIRIT OF OLD WARWICK BEFORE 1788. Attributed to the circle of John Richards, the painting shows homely details such as charity schoolboys, clad in blue and orange regulation issue, descending the steps and washing hanging on a line. Now in a private local collection this oil-painting fascinates me. (Photograph by Simon Photography, Warwick)

In the 1554 Charter, the Corporation was granted the Cross Tavern, situated on the site of the present Courthouse. In 1576 this grant was confirmed as the town had lost the use of the Guildhall in 1571.

Various parts of the building were leased out to shopkeepers and although the building survived the Great Fire of Warwick in 1694, the Mayor's Parlour was slightly damaged and the building began to look very dilapidated.

The rebuilding, which took place from 1724 -31, was expensive and there was insufficient money coming from King Henry VIII's Estate to pay the £2,254 needed so the Corporation took out a massive loan. When the official complaint was made to Chancery in 1737, it was said that the Corporation had indulged in unnecessary feasting and had erected stately buildings of no use to the inhabitants! When Sequestration Orders were issued, it was said that the Corporation owed over £4,000 and until this debt was discharged in 1769 the Corporation was not allowed to manage their affairs or meet in the Court House, which was ironic.

In the later 18th and early 19th centuries, the main assembly room of the Court

THE COURT HOUSE FLOODLIT IN 1932. The lamp standard which carried electricity for the trams until 1930 is clearly visible, and Pridays' (later Tompkins') the corner shop on the left holds many memories for me. I recall an uncomfortable day in 1949 when my school uniform was purchased. As I was tall with a large head, nothing would fit properly, especially the regulation felt, pork-pie hat! In recent years, grants have been given by King Henry VIII's Charity towards the floodlighting of certain Warwick buildings. (Reproduced by permission of Warwickshire County Record Office)

House was the scene of many entertainments frequented by the fashionable society of the County. Balls, lectures and concerts took place under cut glass chandeliers.

For centuries the Magistrates (Borough) Court had been held in the building (as the name implies) and this took place in the room which is now the Council Chamber. After 1836 the Court House was handed over to the Council, but for many years the Charity of King Henry VIII had an obligation to help keep the building in repair.

In recent times several grants have been made to assist repairs, decoration and refurbishment. In 1993 a grant was made towards new furniture for the council chamber which seemed most appropriate as for over a century all decisions concerning the Charity of King Henry VIII were made by the old Corporation in the same building.

The Market Hall (Museum)

Built in 1670 by William Hurlbutt and paid for by public subscription, because the old Booth Hall was felt to be inconvenient, this distinctive building originally had open arcaded sides on the ground floor. The hall was built on stone pillars and in the centre of the ground floor masonry was a small "L" shaped lock-up known as the "Black Hole". This dark space, with no drains, measured only 14 feet by 4 feet and as many as 13 people awaiting trial by the local magistrates had been imprisoned there at any one time. It was in use until 1846 when repeated complaints by the Court Leet eventually resulted in the building of a new lock-up in Theatre Street.

Interestingly this same space still remains, today occupied by boilers. Recently I was able to peep inside and some graffiti scratched onto the stone wall in the 18th century is still visible.

The upper floors of the Market Hall were let to tradesmen such as leatherworkers, but also plays and wild beast shows were performed there. The Corporation Accounts for 1726-7 include "*Received … for the show of the lyon and leopard and for the poppet show £1 5sh 6d.*"

Dr William Allan, the present Curator of the Museum, told me recently that a few years ago when some floor boards were being taken up, an old play bill dating from the mid 18th century was found. Entitled "The Provok'd Wife" the play by Sir John Vanbrugh sounded interesting! Also near to Dr Allan's office the remains of an old hatchway were found which were believed to date from the 18th century when the building was used by the local Militia to store weapons.

In 1836 the Warwickshire Natural History and Archaeological Society was formed, rooms were rented in the Market Hall and by 1840 the entire upper section of the hall was being used. Many of the prominent inhabitants joined the new Society and the members included Elizabeth Savage Landor (sister of the poet and then living in Landor House), Richard Child Heath, Edward Wood of Newbold Revel and many more.

Warwick bookseller, William Groves Perry (1796-1863) and Rev. W.T. Bree were

*THE MARKET HALL CLEARLY LABELLED "MUSEUM" AND THE MARKET
SQUARE AS IT WAS AROUND 1910. Looking rather run down and minus the
attractive cupola and balustrade which were only restored in 1965, the Museum building
was still owned by King Henry VIII Charity at this time. As a matter of interest, the
fountain in the middle of the square was demolished in the 1960s, but to this day there is
still speculation as to what exactly happened to the stones. (Reproduced by permission of
Warwickshire County Museum)*

joint curators of the herbarium and a collection of botanical specimens was built up,
each carefully mounted on card and labelled. When Perry died, his own collection
was purchased by the Society and although now in store, these specimens still form
part of the Museum's collection today.

The Rev. Peter Bellinger Brodie, Vicar of Rowington, was a well known geologist
and from 1853 to his death in 1897 he did much to assist geological study in
Warwickshire. There were a number of clergymen and doctors actively connected
with the Society including the influential Canon Young, Rector of Whitnash, who
together with his friend Dr Baker, a retired surgeon living in Leamington, in 1874
compiled a catalogue of plants to be found in Warwickshire.

By 1900 however, the Society had few members and William Bevington Gibbins
of Ettington, a Quaker philanthropist who was President for a number of years,
financed many activities himself, including the rearrangement of the displays.

In 1932 the Society offered the entire collection to the Warwickshire County
Council which thus became the first county in Britain to take charge of a Museum
service.

INFLUENTIAL CANON J.R. YOUNG, RECTOR OF WHITNASH FROM 1846-1884 was a keen member of the Warwick Natural History and Archaelogical Society which rented rooms in the Market Hall. Having joined in 1848, Canon Young later became a Committee Member and he furthered the cause of science by encouraging the pupils in his prep school to learn about botany, entomology and new inventions. Many future Members of Parliament attended his school at Whitnash Rectory and he also became well-known as an amateur printer. (Reproduced by permission of Clwyd Record Office)

THE UPPER ROOM OF THE MARKET HALL IN 1916 WHEN IT WAS USED TO DISPLAY MUSEUM EXHIBITS. Although I knew it was built in 1670 by William Hurlbutt, I did not fully appreciate the age of the Market Hall until recently when I saw these huge beams in the upper room. Now used as a working area by Museum staff, the restoration of dormer windows in 1965 has given more light to this most interesting area. (Reproduced by permission of Warwickshire County Museum)

However the future of the Market Hall itself was still unsure. The Trustees of King Henry VIII Charity wanted to sell it to the County Council as it was costly to maintain, but many townspeople were in favour of the Museum having purpose-built premises. However, E.G. Tibbits sprang to the defence of the old building. Newly appointed a Trustee to the Charity of King Henry VIII, he organised the opposition and soon the Market Hall was safe from demolition; in 1936 it was scheduled as an Ancient Monument.

In 1938 the Charity Trustees handed over the building and the County officially took charge of the Market Hall, providing certain conditions were met. However because of the Second World War and time taken for repairs it was not until 1951 that the refurbished Museum finally opened. Since then the Museum has gone from strength to strength and today the Curator Dr Allan has a staff of around a dozen to assist him, including a biologist, an ecologist, designers, clerical assistants and various volunteers. The keeper of biology, Pamela Copson, recently showed me some specimens from 19th century herbariums. Her enthusiasm for her subject was highly infectious as she described her 25 years of service; her working area being close to some enormous old wooden beams, which serve as reminders of the great antiquity of the building, so much connected with the Charity of King Henry VIII.

The Butt Yard and The Butts Cottages

There are so many interesting properties once owned by King Henry VIII's Charity that a book could be filled with descriptions of them. However in this book I have been forced to be selective, but there is one more site which is particularly interesting.

In the 16th century the Buttyard where archery was practised, was situated close

MR J.H. FALLEN AND MRS COPSON PICTURED IN 1929. Mr Fallen was the caretaker of the King's High School from 1915 until 1945 and long-serving Mrs Copson was a domestic assistant from 1912. Both lived in the cottages in The Butts then owned by King Henry VIII's Charity. Mr Fallen at number 19 and Mrs Copson in number 21. Still remembered in Warwick today as being a great character, Mr Fallen became the caretaker of the Preparatory School in the Butts in 1945 and he continued until a few years before his death in 1959. (King's High School Archives)

to Eastgate, within the town walls. In the Book of John Fisher there was mention of payments in 1580 for new rails and posts *"for St Mary's Buttes"*, following an official inspection. At the end of the 18th century, cottages were built on the site of this Buttyard and they too have quite an interesting history.

Owned by King Henry VIII's Charity until they were sold to the Warwick Schools Foundation in the 1970s, these cottages were inhabited during much of the 20th century by several employees of the King's High School For Girls. The long serving caretaker Mr Fallen lived at number 19 for many years and next door lived Mrs Copson, employed by the school in a domestic role.

Although small and now mostly in need of modernisation, these cottages are full of interesting features. On the detailed Health Map of 1851 they appear as most desirable residences, each served by a water house and privy in the back garden.

ST MARY'S AND OTHER CHURCHES

In many ways the property, privileges and obligations formerly connected with St Mary's Collegiate Church formed the basic part of the Estate of King Henry VIII in Warwick.

General Background

It would appear that St Mary's Church owed much to the patronage of the various rulers of Warwick Castle from Saxon times onward.

Founded in Saxon times and first mentioned in 1086 in the Domesday Book when it held one hide of land at Myton, in 1183 St Mary's was united with the Collegiate Church of All Saints which had previously existed within the castle grounds. Earl Roger de Newburgh endowed St Mary's with land and property including the church of St Nicholas in Warwick (also the other smaller churches of St Michael, St Lawrence and others) various houses in and around Warwick and also numerous tithes.

Around 1367 other smaller churches in Warwick were closed, the inhabitants being told to attend St Mary's or St Nicholas' and Thomas Beauchamp, Earl of Warwick from 1329 to 1369, demolished the old Norman church of St Mary's and began to build a far grander one. Thomas inherited much property in the Worcestershire village of Chaddesley Corbett and this he gave to St Mary's Church, to help pay for the rebuilding. Only the crypt remains today of the Norman church and appropriately the tomb of Thomas Beauchamp still remains in the chancel. The next Earl of Warwick, Thomas Beauchamp II, completed the work which his father had begun and by his death in 1401, much of the rebuilding had been finished.

The famous Richard Beauchamp, Earl of Warwick from 1401-1439 (one of the wealthiest Englishmen of his time) left many valuable gifts to St Mary's including property and golden treasures, in order to pay for the building of the Beauchamp Chapel and the stipends of priests to chant masses there. Richard's splendid tomb is amongst the finest in England and today still dominates the Beauchamp Chapel.

In 1544 St Mary's voluntarily gave up its possessions but in 1545 when King Henry VIII's Charity was granted to Warwick, most of these were granted back to the town with the Corporation acting as the Trustees. This meant that the Corporation, and after 1836 the Trustees, acted as the lay rector of four parishes… St Mary's, St Nicholas', Budbrooke and Chaddesley Corbett. However as the Charity Trustees were allowed to have the Great tithes in these four parishes, they were also liable for the upkeep of the chancel in all four places until 1936, when remaining tithes and chancel responsibilities were phased out.

From 1545 the Charity of King Henry VIII was responsible for the payment of the stipend of the vicars of St Mary, St Nicholas and Budbrooke (in latter years augmenting the stipend if there was insufficient income) although the Crown generally appointed the vicar of St Mary's. There has also been a general obligation to provide suitable residences for the vicars and in the case of St Mary's to pay stipends of certain other church officers. Before 1836 the Corporation had these liabilities, but from then on the Trustees of the Charity took on the obligations.

The Vicars and Their Stipends

In 1545 the stipends of the vicars were
>The Vicar of St Mary's ... £20 per annum
>The Vicar of St Nicholas ... £13 6sh 8d
>The Vicar of Budbrooke ... £5 3sh 4d

Payments were also made to two chaplains at St Mary's who received £6 13sh 4d each, the Clerk at St Mary's who received £3 6sh 8d and the sexton at St Mary's who had £2.

From time to time, these payments were increased and sometimes the positions varied or the same man held two or more posts. However as might be imagined, the matter of salaries was a constant source of friction between the Corporation (who wished to pay as little as possible because they always said there was insufficient profit from King Henry VIIIs Estate) and the clergy who often demanded what they considered to be their due.

Members of the Corporation were bound by their oath to attend morning service at St Mary's and from 1545 they occupied the pews previously designated for the Dean and Canons. The Corporation could be fined for non-attendance and more than one vicar took advantage of this to harangue the Corporation from the pulpit. Some farcical situations occurred when Aldermen sitting grandly in their official robes were forced to listen politely to criticism during the sermon.

In 1618 Rev Thomas Hall, vicar of St Mary's, thus angered the Corporation who protested against his "invective sermons and reproachful and scandalous speeches against the Bailiff and Burgesses". Eventually matters were sorted out and Mr Hall's stipend was increased as he asked, but there must have been some lively church services before that.

From time to time, increases in stipend were forced upon the Corporation and in 1637 the amounts rose to £70 for the vicar of St Mary's, £30 for his assistant, £50 for the vicar of St Nicholas, £21 18sh for the vicar of Budbrooke, £5 6sh 8d for the clerk of St Mary's and £3 for the sexton.

In 1816 the amounts were dramatically increased after the clergy and some town officials made a petition to Chancery. The stipends were in some cases doubled and went up from £135 to £250 for the vicar of St Mary's, from £60 to £105 for his assistant, from £100 to £200 for the vicar of St Nicholas, from £56 18sh to £100 for the vicar of Budbrooke, from £11 6sh 8d to £20 for the clerk of St Mary's and from £6 10sh to £10 16sh for the sexton.

Many of the Vicars acted as personal chaplains to the Earl. John Boudier, vicar from 1815 to 1873, was Domestic Chaplain to the Earl, Rural Dean and an Honorary Canon of Worcester Cathedral, Warwick then being in the Diocese of Worcester. Thurston Rivington began as vicar of St Nicholas in 1884 but transferred to St Mary's in 1899. He was also Domestic Chaplain to the Earl and an Honorary Canon of Worcester Cathedral.

THE REV. JOHN BOUDIER, VICAR OF ST MARY'S FROM 1815 TO 1872, IN THE VICARAGE GARDEN AROUND 1860. Now known as The Deanery, the vicarage was owned and maintained by King Henry VIII's Charity until the 1970s when the present modern vicarage was built nearby and the former dwelling sold. In John Boudier's time, a straight path led from the vicarage garden across the north side of the churchyard to St Mary's Church. (Reproduced by permission of Warwickshire County Museum)

The Provision of Suitable Vicarages

The Corporation was supposed to provide suitable houses for the clergy and in the 16th and 17th centuries, the vicar of St Mary's had a vicarage in the Old Square in Warwick. This house was burned down in the Fire of Warwick in 1694 and rebuilt afterwards. In 1768 the house was exchanged for The Deanery in The Butts and this building still remains. In 1971 part of it known as The Glebe House was leased out and Mrs Ethel Brown, a well known local Town Councillor and a Warwick Schools Governor (Chairman of KHSW and Mayor in 1970-1971) became the tenant. Later the Old Deanery was sold and the modern vicarage built in 1976. This house, close to the stone arch in The Butts is now the only vicarage directly maintained by the Charity.

Chancel and Church Repairs

Until 1637, the Corporation was merely responsible for the upkeep of the chancel of the four churches (St Mary's, St Nicholas', Budbrooke and Chaddesley Corbett) but following the decree of Lord Keeper Coventry, the responsibilities included the main part of the church of St Mary's.

THIS SHOWS THE ST MARY'S CHURCH BUILDING IN WHICH THOMAS OKEN, JOHN FISHER AND THE OTHER EARLY CORPORATION MEMBERS WORSHIPPED. Architecturally the church was most interesting, being built largely in the 14th century, apart from the Beauchamp Chapel (shown to the right) which was built in the 15th century. In 1694 the tower and nave were destroyed in the Great Fire of Warwick and rebuilding took place in the 10 years which followed. (Reproduced by permission of Warwickshire County Record Office)

THIS ENGRAVING BY FREDERICK WHITEHEAD SHOWS ST MARY'S CHURCH UNDER SCAFFOLDING IN 1885-6. Many repairs to the stonework were then necessary and a new clock was installed in the tower in 1902. The chimes which had so impressed the American writer Nathanial Hawthorne ("Our Old Home" 1864) were repaired in 1902 and today similar chimes ring out such tunes as "The Bluebells of Scotland", "Home Sweet Home" or "Warwickshire Lads and Lasses" at certain times of the day. (Reproduced by permission of Warwickshire County Record Office)

Also the rector of a parish (i.e. the Corporation in Warwick) besides being given the tithes, was reminded of the obligation to give some of the proceeds towards church maintenance and poor relief.

Not only did the Great Fire have a disastrous effect on the town of Warwick, but the 300 year old St Mary's church was badly damaged. The tower, nave, and transepts were destroyed and the chancel roof and stalls were damaged, although the Beauchamp Chapel largely escaped thanks to a gang of firefighters, probably organised by James Fish Senior, the Parish Clerk. They stopped the fire at the Chapel doorway, which was rebuilt afterwards by a local mason Samuel Dunckley.

There was no way that King Henry VIII's Estate could pay for rebuilding and a nation wide subscription fund was launched for Warwick and St Mary's Church.

The architect of the new building was William Wilson of Sutton Coldfield and the masons were William and Francis Smith, later to be important members of the Corporation, with Francis Smith being responsible for the rebuilding of the Court House. The new church seems to have gone according to plan until the tower created serious problems, which were only resolved when the advice of Edward Strong, (a master mason who had worked on St Pauls in London) and Sir Christopher Wren was sought. Mr Strong and his son visited Warwick and a modified plan involving the tower being built of harder stone, partly out into the roadway was adopted.

The highly skilled metalworker Nicholas Paris who had already carried out re-gilding of Richard Beauchamp's tomb when the Beauchamp Chapel was restored in the 1680s, did much work in the new church, including making the ornate iron railings round Robert Dudley's tomb. In 1702 the chancel was restored; the Corporation paying £50 from King Henry VIII's Estate and the rest coming from the Warwick Fire Fund to which Queen Anne had given £1,000.

In January 1852 fifty men were employed in the chancel scraping the walls and completing restoration work.

In 1857 the church was closed for a time whilst renovation work was carried out including the demolition of the old high reading desk. In 1885 scaffolding was erected round St Mary's tower whilst much restoration work went on and in the early 1890s the Charity Trustees had to provide the chancel with a new roof.

For many years of the 20th century, the profits from King Henry VIII Charity were insufficient for the traditional demands and money from the diocese and other sources made up the deficiency. However in recent times increased profits from the Charity have meant that work at St Mary's has been paid for once again by money from King Henry VIII's Charity.

THE MEMORIAL TO THOMAS OKEN AND HIS WIFE JOAN IS SITUATED NEAR TO THE REGIMENTAL CHAPEL IN ST MARY'S CHURCH. As he was keen on civic matters and improvements, I think Oken would have been amused to see that a fire-extinguisher is situated close to his memorial. (Photograph by Simon Photography, Warwick)

A Walk Around St Mary's Church

1) Burial Vaults and the Crypt

In no way should this chapter be treated as a guide book to St Mary's or any of the other churches, but mention of various items which can be seen on a tour around the church as it is today will help to explain certain facts concerned with the Charity of King Henry VIII in the past.

It is worthwhile to recall that the crypt, chancel, vestry, Chapter House, and Beauchamp Chapel all survived the Great Fire in 1694 and would have been known to Thomas Oken and the other Corporation members who took control of the Charity of King Henry VIII in 1545. Over the centuries the surface trappings may have altered but the basic structures are little altered.

Near the entrance to the vestry is the memorial to Thomas Oken who died in 1573, and his wife Joan; their brasses being rescued from the fire in 1694. I often

THE CRYPT OF ST MARY'S CHURCH IS ALL THAT REMAINS OF THE NORMAN BUILDING ERECTED IN THE 12TH CENTURY. There is a wonderful atmosphere amongst these sandstone pillars and for the past couple of years volunteers, led by Michael and Bess Ashmore, have served tea, coffee and biscuits to grateful visitors. Crypts of all kinds fascinate me, but St Mary's Crypt is particularly special and I have had many interesting conversations with visitors and helpers whilst lingering over my coffee. (JF)

wish that Oken's memorial was situated in a more noticeable position, but in his will he asked that he should be buried near to the Chapel of St Ann and this spot is as near as possible to the former chapel.

Once having passed through the vestry door the steep steps to the ancient crypt lie ahead. I cannot use these steps without thinking of my late father for he often used to describe in humorous detail how he had fallen down the entire flight when a boy, being taken on a tour of St Mary's as a birthday treat by his elder sister.

One of the eeriest parts of the church is the stone vaulted chamber situated under the vestry, at the bottom of the steps. Centuries ago this had been known as The Friar's Kitchen and it had probably been a guest room in medieval times. Thomas Kemp describes how from a margin note in a copy of Dugdale's History formerly owned by Francis Hiorne, he learned that Mr Hiorne was the architect who converted the ancient chamber into a burial vault for the Earls of Warwick. Francis Hiorne was very much connected with King Henry VIII's Estate for he was Mayor of Warwick from 1773-4, 1782-3 and 1787-8 and he completed the restoration work on Eastgate in 1788.

A peep through the ornate door into this burial vault is sufficient to send shivers down the spine for a number of sealed coffin shelves can be seen and a chill wind blows through a grille from the churchyard. A macabre chapter of "Moonfleet" by J.Meade Faulkener which I read as a child always springs to mind whenever I peer into this vault and with a little imagination one can think of being in close proximity to the coffin of a long dead earl or countess.

An old friend of mine drily remarked that this burial vault is probably the only piece of Warwick which the present Earl of Warwick now owns. The castle and other local properties were sold decades ago.

Fulke Greville

The octagonal 14th century Chapter House, used by the Dean and Canons prior to 1544, is situated close to the steps to the crypt. However I find that it is difficult to appreciate anything else in the room apart from the enormous tomb to Sir Fulke Greville which is in the centre. The tomb seems far too large for its surroundings and I for one find it singularly unattractive. However Sir Fulke Greville himself was most interesting and he had many dealings with the Corporation and the Estate of King Henry VIII.

Sir Fulke spent £20,000 of his own money on rebuilding Warwick Castle in the early 17th century and because of this he and the Corporation had to entertain King James I in the Lord Leycester Hospital in 1617. There being insufficient spare funds in the Estate of King Henry VIII, the Bailiff and Corporation got heavily into debt over the visit. A cousin and great friend of Sir Philip Sydney, Fulke was a well known poet himself and his poems are sometimes still found in anthologies. As a courtier, he lived much in London and in 1628 the 74 year old nobleman was stabbed to death in his house at Holborn by Ralph Hayward, a servant who afterwards committed suicide with the same weapon. The unusual circumstances have led some

SIR FULKE GREVILLE, FIRST LORD BROOKE AND FRIEND OF QUEEN ELIZABETH I, IS BURIED IN THE CHAPTER HOUSE IN ST MARY'S CHURCH. Born in 1554, the same year as his great friend Sir Philip Sydney, he spent a huge amount of money on the restoration of Warwick Castle which had been granted to him in 1604. He died unmarried in 1628 having been fatally wounded by servant Ralph Hayward in Brooke House, Holborn. (Reproduced by permission of Warwickshire County Record Office)

to suggest that it was in fact a suicide pact between the two men. Fulke took a month to die and 27 days after his death, he was buried under the monument he had planned. He had even penned the touching inscription himself

Fulke Greville
Servant to Queen Elizabeth,
Councillor to King James
And friend to Sir Philip Sidney

Whilst rebuilding was going on, Fulke had used a room in the Watergate Tower in Warwick Castle and this room, believed by many to be haunted, today contains his portrait and details of his life.

The Chancel

As has been explained, this area had special significance for the Trustees of King Henry VIII's Charity because they were specifically liable for its maintenance.

Over the centuries the main tomb in the position of honour in the chancel, that of Thomas Beauchamp I, Earl of Warwick from 1329 to 1369 and his wife Katherine Mortimer, has needed attention and repair. It is a particularly interesting tomb for the figures of 36 grieving relatives are portrayed round the sides and students of medieval costume can learn much from them.

"THE CHANTRY IS A BEAUTIFUL LITTLE APARTMENT WITH RICH FAN-TRACERY VAULTING ...... In this Chapel is an old chest, some helmets and an ancient desk." So wrote Thomas Kemp in 1905 and the chapel does not seem to have changed so much since Edwardian times. Today known as the Dean's Chapel, it is freshly painted and contains a rich altar cloth used in Queen Elizabeth II's Coronation, which was donated by Sir Anthony Eden when he was the local M.P. I find this Victorian picture particularly emotive as it captures the aura of a byegone age. (Reproduced by permission of Warwickshire County Record Office)

Thomas Beauchamp had an interesting life, having fought in the French wars, especially at Crecy in 1346 and Poitiers in 1356 and being the Guardian of the Black Prince. He did much for the town of Warwick, building the Booth Hall and other buildings and it is said that Thomas obtained much money from a ransom of a French Archbishop in the French Wars. He died from fever in Calais in 1369 and his (embalmed?) body was transported back to Warwick.

Near the door from the chancel to the vestry is a small brass and much larger public notice telling of the death of Sir William Parr, the Marquis of Northampton who died in 1571. The death of this nobleman, who was the brother of King Henry VIII's last wife Catherine Parr, when visiting the Priory gave the Corporation many anxious moments. John Fisher in "The Black Book" gave a full description of events and in the end the Corporation were relieved to learn that Queen Elizabeth I herself was prepared to pay the considerable expenses of the funeral in St Mary's.

There are several reminders of Pre-Reformation times in the chancel and it may well have been that some of the parishioners in the 16th and 17th centuries secretly indulged in previous Roman Catholic customs. Two iron rings about 6 feet high can be seen in the wall above the marble sanctuary rails and these once supported the Lenten Veil which was suspended before the high altar until it was rent on Good Friday at the third hour. Another instance of a Pre-Reformation practice is the Easter Sepulchre on the north side of the sanctuary in which bread, consecrated in the Eucharist, was placed on Maundy Thursday. This was continually watched day and night, until Easter Sunday morning in memory of the Resurrection of Christ.

The Beauchamp Chapel

In his will, the wealthy Richard Beauchamp, Earl of Warwick, who died in 1439, left money and directions for the building of the now famous chapel. It was completed in 1464 and consecrated in 1475 around 21 years having been taken by some of the finest craftsmen in England to carry out their tasks.

When the Corporation of 1545 took over responsiblity for St Mary's, the wonderful chapel which attracted numerous pilgrims was only 70 years old and the magnificent gilt and marble tomb of Richard Beauchamp, stood proudly in the centre. I often try to picture the chapel without the dominant tombs of Robert Dudley, Earl of Leycester and Ambrose Dudley, Earl of Warwick, which were

A BEAR AND GRIFFIN LIE AT THE FEET OF THE EFFIGY ON RICHARD BEAUCHAMP'S TOMB IN THE BEAUCHAMP CHAPEL. (JF)

A POPULAR ITEM IN ST MARY'S CHURCH IS THIS BEAR WHICH LIES AT THE FEET OF THE EFFIGY ON THE TOMB OF AMBROSE DUDLEY, EARL OF WARWICK, IN THE BEAUCHAMP CHAPEL. (JF)

added in the later 16th century … it must have been most impressive, with the fine stained glass windows made by John Prudde (King Henry VI's glazier) together with the carved wooden stalls, wall painting and fine altar.

The appearance of the chapel was changed by the construction of the various Dudley tombs in the late 16th century and in 1642 a great deal of damage was done by the Puritans in the Civil War period. Many of them regarded Chantry Chapels for the saying of masses for the dead as horrific places and the Corporation of the time (whose ultimate responsibility it must have been) must have been glad when Lady Katherine Leveson left money known as The Foxley Charity, to help repair and maintain the chapel which had fallen into disrepair by the 1670s.

Prior to this in the mid 17th century, the floor of the Beauchamp Chapel fell in and William Field, minister of the Unitarian Chapel from 1789 to 1843, in his history of "The Town and Castle of Warwick" (published in 1815) described the terrible consequences.

> *"Earl Richard's coffin, being either accidentally broken or purposely unclosed, the body was found perfect and fresh: but on letting in the air, it rapidly fell to decay The Ladies of Warwick had rings and other ornaments made from the hair."*

A spine-chilling story indeed, but I have heard of other similar instances when relics were stolen from famous corpses.

In the 19th century the Beauchamp Chapel attracted many tourists. The Corporation and later the Trustees of King Henry VIII Charity, together with the clergy of St Mary's and the Trustees of other charities which provided maintainence money, kept the chapel in reasonable repair. I particularly like the entry in a small Victorian guide book which I came across recently.

Published in 1882, Bevan's Guide to Warwickshire said,

"On the S. Side of the choir is the Beauchamp Chapel, one of the most exquisite Perpendicular examples in the kingdom (a fee of 6d has to be paid)."

I wonder how many of the visitors today would be prepared to pay an equivalent amount?

By the 1920s more restoration work was necessary and Churchwarden Thomas Kemp and other prominent citizens worked hard to establish a Restoration Fund. In 1924 a Grand Fete was held in the Castle Grounds to raise money for the

ST MARY'S CHURCH BEFORE THE GALLERIES WERE TAKEN DOWN IN 1896. An edition of the Warwick Advertiser in the 1920s carried an amusing article by an elderly ex-choirmaster who recalled that occasionally people dropped things from the galleries onto the heads of unsuspecting worshippers below. (Reproduced by permission of Warwickshire County Record Office)

Beauchamp Chapel Restoration Fund and some necessary work was completed. With smaller profits from King Henry VIII's Charity coming into St Mary's for much of the 20th century, the Chapel received grants from other organisations. In the early 1970s major restoration was carried out so that St Mary's could again be very proud of its unique Chapel.

The Organs

Since Medieval times there has been an organ in St Mary's Church and music has been an important part of worship.

The Medieval organ is believed to have been situated on a stone screen which separated the chancel from the nave, with a second organ on a western gallery in the Beauchamp Chapel. For the first 149 years after the setting up of King Henry VIII's Estate, Corporation money helped to maintain these instruments.

However in the Great Fire of 1694, both were destroyed and Thomas Swarbrick, a skilled organ builder who later moved to Warwick, built another around 1717 which was also positioned between the nave and the chancel. In 1793 this organ was moved to the West End and a new gallery was built, similar to those which already existed for the congregation. In 1864 the organ was moved slightly forward, away from a wall which had been causing damp. The beautifully carved case, which was enlarged in 1896, now houses one section of the present organ.

Following the extensive church restoration of the 1880s, a new electric organ was installed in 1897 by Hope-Jones. It cost £1,245 with an extra £118 for the gas engine in the crypt to supply the wind. This organ was one of the first in the country to have electric action but there were many initial problems. A major rebuild in 1966 by Alfred Davies and Son of Northampton and another in 1973 by Nicholsons of Malvern have resulted in the present arrangement whereby two organs are available, one of them utilising the old Swarbrick case and the other, which is usually used to accompany worship, situated in the transept.

The salary of the organist of St Mary's was often recorded in the Account Books of the Charity and in 1834 he was paid £50 p.a.

St Nicholas' Church

Although often overshadowed by St Mary's the church of St Nicholas is said to be built on a far older ecclesiastical site, where a nunnery sacked by the Danes in 1016 once stood. Having been granted to the Canons of the Collegiate Church of St. Mary, the Corporation was granted the right to appoint the vicars until 1839 when they sold the advowson.

As with St Mary's the Corporation was liable for repairs to the chancel, but as the Earls of Warwick and the Corporation frequented St Mary's, St Nicholas' Church on the whole had a less wealthy congregation, being more like a traditional church in a small country town. The vicar was always paid far less than the vicar of St Mary's and in general there seemed to be a more homely atmosphere.

THIS ENGRAVING BY J. BRANDARD SHOWS THE SOUTH SIDE OF WARWICK IN THE EARLY 19TH CENTURY. St Nicholas' Church is most prominent, adjoining the river meadows which were part of the property owned by the Charity. Today St Nicholas' Park occupies the site of these meadows and the church is largely hidden by trees. (Reproduced by permission of Warwickshire County Record Office)

However many interesting historical facts are associated with the church and Thomas Kemp quotes from old Churchwardens' Accounts how the bier was often sent to the gallows (on Gallows Hill along the Heathcote Lane, within the parish) to fetch the bodies of the prisoners for burial, sometimes tolling the funeral bell for them if payment had been made.

As the building was in poor repair, the church was rebuilt in 1779/80, the tower having been built in 1748. The chancel was replaced in 1869 and various stained glass windows were donated. One of the saddest stories I have ever seen depicted is in a main window in the centre of the north wall. It was erected in 1864 by G. M. Heathcote and Mary his wife in memory of five of their children, the last three dying within eight days. The father and mother are shown weeping over five small coffins.

In recent times there have been many changes in the fabric of the church, in effect turning it into a multi purpose building. In 1976 the chancel was bricked off and toilets constructed, but at that time, the profits from King Henry VIII's Charity were small and the congregation and diocese paid much of the cost. The Church Hall in Gerrard Street was sold to the Castle Hill Baptist Church which was then in need of additional premises and this helped to finance the reconstruction work.

Despite the modern alterations to the church fabric, there are many traditonal items still preserved there. The church boasts the oldest ecclesiastical brass in Warwickshire, that to Rev. Robert Willardsey, the first vicar (previous clerics had been rectors) who died in 1425. This brass has been moved from the vestry and is now to the right of the chancel arch.

On the gallery there is a photograph and memorial to John Lees who was organist and choirmaster for 55 years from 1907-1962. Also a modern window in the nave was designed by Dick Hosking in the 1970s as a memorial to Mr Lees.

Traditionally there was a vicarage in St Nicholas Church Street, close to the church and this house was rebuilt in 1819-20, King Henry VIII's charity being liable for repairs. In modern times however, with reorganisation of the Parishes of St Mary and St Nicholas, the old vicarage has been sold, a modern house on the enormous Woodloes Estate being considered more appropriate for one of the present team vicars.

Budbrooke

As with St Mary's and St Nicholas' from 1545 the Corporation had the responsibility for the chancel and paying the stipend of the vicar. Traditionally St Michael's Church had been administered from St Mary's Collegiate Church after Roger, Earl of Warwick, gave the church to the Canons of St Mary's in 1123. In 1545 the Corporation of Warwick was granted the living of Budbrooke as part of King Henry VIII's Charity.

Budbrooke Church is an interesting building with a Norman Doorway (now blocked off) which is visible from the churchyard and inside the nave. The chancel and tower are mostly 14th century and there is a large memorial to Roland Dormer, Baron Wing who died in 1712 which Pevsner refers to as being *"outstandingly good."* Grove Park House which was within a couple of miles of the church, was the traditional residence of the Lords Dormer and there are references to various members of the family within the church.

Mrs Elsie Richardson who has done much research into the history told me recently that some years ago two vaults were discovered during restoration inside the church. One vault, about six feet deep and containing two coffins, was near the door and the other vault was in the transept.

The churchyard is full of interest as until 1960 the Barracks of the Royal Warwickshire Regiment were close by. There are many memorials to ex-soldiers who were interred in the churchyard and lines of colourful metal crosses, recently refurbished by boys from Warwick School, and the later smooth white headstones,

BUDBROOKE PARISH CHURCH, DEDICATED TO ST MICHAEL, IS SITUATED ON A HILL ABOUT HALF A MILE FROM THE MODERN VILLAGE OF HAMPTON MAGNA AND CLOSE TO THE WARWICK TO BIRMINGHAM RAILWAY LINE. In medieval times the main village was near the church but this settlement was abandoned and Hampton on the Hill became more important. Today this interesting church is rather isolated, except for the vicarage and a few houses, including Grange Farm, which is still owned by King Henry VIII Charity. (JF)

tell a sad story. The memorials of youngsters such as Private H.W. Turner who died in 1914 at the age of 17 and that of Boy Soldier W.H. Moore who died in 1943 at the age of 16, make sombre reading. Also in the churchyard is the distinctive antelope weather-vane from the Barracks and the Victorian font (buried for protection) which was felt to be superfluous inside the church. Amongst the gravestones I spotted one marking the grave of William and Bessie Fretwell, my great uncle and his wife, whom I never met, but whose memorial gave me added interest in Budbrooke and its church.

Chaddesley Corbett

As with the other churches, the Corporation of Warwick as Lay Rector was responsible for the repair of the chancel of St Cassian's Church in Chaddesley Corbett. The tithes were paid to the Corporation who were supposed to grant a certain amount towards church repairs and the relief of the poor.

In 1545 the Corporation was granted the advowson of the church and also that of Rushock and Stone nearby, as these parishes had traditionally belonged to the Canons of St Mary's, but in 1637 this advowson was removed from the Corporation.

The ancient church of St Cassian (a Grade I Listed Building) is a most interesting one being one of the few churches anywhere in the country to be dedicated to this obscure saint. It is not even known which St Cassian was intended … was it the schoolmaster from Imola in Italy who was killed by his own pupils or perhaps more likely a Greek saint known for his pure living? Parts of the nave date back to around 1150 and the unusual stone font was made around 1160. The chancel dates to the 14th century and is well preserved, as is the 13th century chapel to St Nicholas nearby. Restoration and enlargements took place in the 13th and 14th centuries and it was in 1394 that St Mary's Warwick was granted the patronage. The tower and spire were rebuilt in 1778 and in 1863-4 much restoration work was done in the building.

In St Nicholas' Chapel there are several memorials including an impressive one to Sir Humphrey Packington of nearby Harvington Hall, who was mentioned in some of the leases of Warwick Corporation land. After most of the property in Chaddesley Corbett had been sold and any remaining tithes phased out, the links between the church and Warwick gradually ceased.

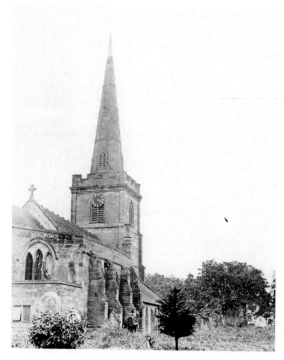

CHADDESLEY CORBETT CHURCH IN WORCESTERSHIRE IN 1892. The original of this photograph, along with other interesting prints, is contained in the photograph album of Thomas Kemp of Warwick, now in Warwickshire County Record Office. (Reproduced by permission of Warwickshire County Record Office)

WARWICK SCHOOL

One of the most fascinating parts of the history of the Charity of King Henry VIII is the story of Warwick School. From 1545 until 1875, the school was an integral part of the Charity, but the foundation of the school is far older than that.

In 1545 Warwick School was mentioned in the Letters Patent which set up King Henry VIII's Charity and so it was always assumed that King Henry VIII had founded the Grammar School. On a memorial in St Mary's Church to Rev. Innes who died in 1842, it was stated that he was *"Headmaster of King Henry VIII's School in this borough for 50 years"* and the Tudor Arms were placed on the Myton Road buildings when they were constructed in 1879.

This assumption went on until 1906 when A.F. Leach wrote "A History of Warwick School" in which he described long forgotten documents confirming the continuous existence of the school from the time of Edward the Confessor (1042-1066). Delighted Old Warwickians donated a statue of Edward the Confessor which still remains in the foyer of Warwick School. However further research has revealed that, beyond reasonable doubt, Warwick School is far older and was founded in 914 by Ethelfled (often called Ethelfleda), the famous Lady of the Mercians, when she established a burh at Warwick as part of a string of fortified Midlands towns, strong enough to stand against repeated Viking onslaughts.

Don Stansbury, author of a recent book on Ethelfled (daughter of the legendary King Alfred) wrote in a letter to me recently, *"I think it probable that Ethelfled established a school when she founded the burh at Warwick. She was doing in Mercia what her father had done in Wessex and we know that educational provision was an important element in Alfred's system."*

When she established a burh, Ethelfled organised a complete small town, with defences, a church and a school. Thus in Warwick the existing Church of All Saints within the Castle precincts was empowered to run a school for boys and this continued until the Collegiate Church of All Saints was amalgamated with the Collegiate Church of St Mary around 1123.

The school continued to be administered by the Collegiate Church of St Mary, with one of the clergy acting as tutor, until 1545 when it became incorporated in the Charity set up by King Henry VIII.

OLD WARWICKIAN SIDNEY FLAVEL JUNIOR 1847-1931. Chairman of the local factory which still bears the family name of Flavels, Sidney Flavel was Mayor of Leamington 6 times, an Alderman for nearly 60 years and also a Freeman of Leamington. As O.W. President in 1924 he unveiled the statue of Edward the Confessor in the foyer of Warwick School and he was a Governor of The Middle School and Warwick School, besides being an original member of Warwickshire County Council. He died at his home in Bushberry Lodge, Willes Road, Leamington Spa in 1931. (Royal Leamington Spa Art Gallery and Museum, Warwick District Council Museum Service)

Mostly Latin and Greek 1545-1875

The letters patent of 1545 which set up King Henry VIII's Charity included the passages,

"Led by the singular love and affection with which we are no little moved to the youthful subjects of our kingdom in the county of Warwick ... do by the tenor of these presents in fact and fully create, erect, found, ordain, make and establish to endure for all future times, a Free School in the said town of Warwick."

The school was referred to in the document as *"The King's New Schole of Warwyke"* and the schoolmaster was to be appointed by the Crown.

In earlier times, the Grammar School had used the disued Church of St John in the Market Square, but in 1545, the dining room of the Warwick Guild (presumably the ground floor room at the Lord Leycester Hospital, now used for functions) was the schoolroom.

After using St Peter's Chapel over Eastgate for a time when the Earl of Leycester had taken over the Guildhall complex, the school returned to its previous premises in St John's Church in the Market Square.

During the Fire of Warwick in 1694, this building was destroyed and in 1699 the original premises of the Vicar's Choral of St Mary's (half-timbered fifteenth century

THE PICTURESQUE OLD COLLEGE IN THE BUTTS WHICH WAS DEMOLISHED IN 1882. Said to have been rebuilt around 1460 from money left by Richard Beauchamp (1401-39) it was once the College of the Vicar's Choral of St Mary's Church. The premises were bought by Warwick Corporation in 1699 to house the King's Grammar School which remained there until 1879. Architecturally almost as old and interesting as the Lord Leycester Hospital, the half-timbered buildings were grouped round a courtyard and their needless demolition was a great loss to the town. (Reproduced by permission of Warwickshire County Record Office)

buildings somewhat similar to the Lord Leycester Hospital) in the Butts were purchased from a local landowner, Sir Thomas Wagstaffe of Tachbrook Mallory, for the sum of £260. For the next 180 years the school occupied these picturesque premises, only leaving in 1879 when the present buildings in the Myton Road were constructed.

As Grammar Schools were not intended to be elementary schools, boys were expected to be literate when they became pupils. Tuition consisted largely of Latin and Greek and important subjects currently studied in today's schools such as Mathematics, Science, English, Geography and French were rarely included, if at all.

The schoolmaster was always a clergyman of the Church of England and he sometimes held other posts as well, for instance that of one of the vicars of St Mary's. From 1616 onwards provision was made for an usher or assistant master, but the position was not always filled.

Until the mid nineteenth century, Warwick School seems to have been a typical old foundation Grammar School, with a fluctuating number of pupils, but never more than one or two masters could easily manage. It was administered directly by Warwick Corporation as Trustees of King Henry VIII's Charity and in 1701 the Corporation ruled that tuition was only to be free to those boys born in Warwick or to those whose parents had lived in the town for 7 years. Until the mid twentieth century, preferential treatment in the form of lower fees was granted to pupils living within the Borough of Warwick, in the continuation of this philosophy.

The early eighteenth century was a time of renewed interest in learning (this was the period when the Bablake Charity School became established in Eastgate) and Warwick School flourished, especially when in 1729 Fulke Weale, a wealthy woollen draper, left a considerable estate for the benefit of the school and university entrants. Two young men, natives of Warwick, were to be maintained and educated at Warwick School and later at university, and over the years this trust increased in value.

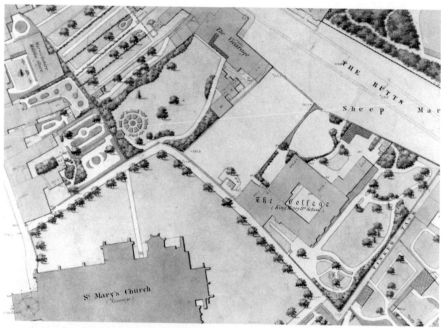

PART OF THE 1851 HEALTH MAP OF THE TOWN SHOWING THE POSITION OF THE COLLEGE BUILDING USED BY WARWICK SCHOOL FROM 1699 TO 1879. The distinctive large stone arch which still remains in The Butts is to the left of the "S" of Sheep Market and the actual site of the college (demolished in 1882) is now occupied by the college garden and the garden of the new vicarage. (Reproduced by permission of Warwickshire County Record Office)

Some Headmasters of Warwick School Prior to Re-organisation

1565-1577 Rev. Ralph Griffin (Also Master of Lord Leycester Hospital from 1571). Salary then £10 per year.

1577-1593 Rev. Humfrey Waring (Also vicar of St Nicholas).

1595 -1620 Rev. John Owen (famous nationwide for Latin epigrams. Buried in old St Pauls' Cathedral, London). Salary was increased to £20 p.a. in 1616.

1633-1648 Rev. Thomas Dugard (Had Parliamentary sympathies? Retired to Barford Rectory 1648. Buried in Barford). Salary was increased to £30 per annum in 1638.

1687-1697 Rev. William Eades (Vicar of St Mary's. Huge arguments with Corporation as Eades thought to sympathise with Roman Catholicism and the Jacobite cause. After 1690 Eades was forced to give up many school responsibilities).

1702-1730 Rev. Richard Lydiate (School very successful).

1730-1762 Rev. Francis Lydiate (Richard's second son born 1709. From 1743 he was also vicar of Budbrooke. Buried St Mary's 1762. At this time the school was highly successful).

1763-1793 Rev. Roberts (unsatisfactory and the Corporation tried, unsuccessfully, to remove him from office. Salary increased to £75 in 1779).

1793-1842 Rev. George Innes (inherited few pupils. Stayed too long. Salary increased from £75 to £135 p.a. in 1818).

1842-1876 Rev. Herbert Hill (inherited few pupils, but very successful). Salary increased to £200 p.a.

George Innes as Headmaster

In his book "A History of Warwick School" published in 1906, A.F. Leach includes an entertaining section describing the 1830s when George Innes was headmaster ... largely the reminiscences of Rev. James Baly, Archdeacon of Calcutta, who contributed to the school magazine 'The Portcullis' in 1900 and 1902.

The headmaster Rev. Innes was thus described:

"He was a venerable, scholarly-looking gentleman ... he was seated in a large invalid's chair, and supported one leg on a 'rest', the foot encased in wraps of large dimensions, such as I had never seen before; in a word, he was suffering from gout ...

Mr Innes was an exceedingly kind and gentle old man. When he met us in the street he not infrequently treated us to a Bath bun, or gave us the coppers to treat ourselves at the then well-known confectioner's shop kept by Miss Harris, a Quaker lady ... Bookbinding and playing the violoncello were his hobbies; the latter was rather a solemn and mournful sound as it reached the school, but his bookbinding was excellent."

SHOWN HERE IN A MODERN PHOTOGRAPH, THE TINKERTANK WALKWAY WAS SOMETIMES THE SCENE OF SCUFFLES BETWEEN BOYS OF THE KING'S GRAMMAR SCHOOL AND THOSE OF THE BABLAKE CHARITY SCHOOL HELD OVER EASTGATE. One pupil recalled that one day around 1835 a large group of perhaps 45 Bablake boys, clad in their old-fashioned blue coats and orange breeches, marched menacingly up the Tinkertank. The Grammar School boys (far fewer in number) expected a fight, but discretion prevailed and after exchanging insults all departed peacefully. (JF)

The school hours as described by Rev. Baly were only 10.30 to 11.30 a.m. every day and 2.30 to 3.15 p.m. three afternoons a week, so the few boys who attended (varying in number between 3 and 18) had plenty of time for play. The only problem was that many years before the playground had been taken over to provide the headmaster with a kitchen garden, so the boys had to play in St Mary's churchyard, often running races of various kinds such as steeplechases over the gravestones and sometimes longer races round the entire churchyard walk, encompassing part of Church Street.

I find the descriptions given by Rev. Baly of life in Warwick School from 1832 to 1838 quite fascinating and modern school life seems quite dull by comparison. Not only did the boys play over and among the graves but the Archdeacon decribed how they *"acquired a slight and crude knowledge of osteology by handling quantities of bones which were thrown out when graves were dug ... When we pelted him (the gravedigger) with the bones he had 'spaded' out, it was 'awful' to hear anathemas of a most personal character emerge from the earth, accompanied by promises of such a dreadful nature, as he shouted 'Oi! I know who you be,' etc."*

Rev. Innes continued as headmaster till he died in July 1842 aged 82.

Rev. Herbert Hill (1842 to 1876)

This efficient and kindly man did much for Warwick School and during his time as Headmaster boarding was again possible (Innes had discontinued it) and the number of day boys increased sharply.

Rev. Hill was married to Bertha, the daughter of the poet Robert Southey and they had eight children. Whilst in Rugby, prior to being appointed to Warwick, Herbert Hill had been tutor to Tom and Matthew Arnold (the well known poet) who were the sons of Dr Arnold, headmaster of Rugby school. At least once the poet Wordsworth came to stay in the schoolhouse in Warwick and the Hills counted various literary figures amongst their personal friends.

After the scheme for re-organisation of the King's Schools had been produced in 1875, Herbert Hill retired, somewhat unwillingly, the following year. His wife died in 1877 and in 1880 he became Master of the Lord Leycester Hospital, which position he held until shortly before his death in 1892.

The King's Schools Scheme is Set Up in 1875

By the mid 19th century educational matters were to the forefront nationwide and although it was agreed that the school needed to expand with a modernised curriculum, conflicting ideas made decisions difficult.

The result was that in 1875 the King's Schools' Foundation was set up ... three schools were to replace the old Grammar School and because there was no way that King Henry VIII's Estate could fund this alone, various other charities were amalgamated into the new scheme. Almost all the charities in Warwick gave annual donations or made some major contribution and a few children of the town were able to benefit from scholarships.

THE FRONT OF WARWICK SCHOOL IN 1902. Little different from the view from the Chapel side today this was one of a series of photographs in an official album. (RHT)

Three secondary schools were set up ... firstly a King's (Grammar) School for 250 boys (70 boarders) run on broadly traditional lines in new premises in the Myton Road; secondly a King's Middle School for 100 boys with a modern curriculum in new premises in The Butts and thirdly The Kings High School For Girls, the counterpart of the boys' Middle School and catering for 80 girls, in Landor House which had been given by the Trustees of Ann Johnson's Charity. The fees for the Grammar School were to be £6 -£12 per year, whilst those of the Middle School and the Girls' School were to be £2 -£4 per year.

There were conflicting fortunes for the new schools. The Boys' Grammar School struggled at times because it charged higher fees than the Middle School and in 1906 the sensible decision was taken to amalgamate the two boys schools on the Myton Road site, the name eventually being changed to Warwick School. Despite the cramped site, the girls' school flourished and soon became one of the foremost schools in the Midlands.

In the 20th century, both boys' and girls' schools had the benefit of County money in return for a number of free places for some of the brightest children in the area. Following the 1944 Education Act, Warwick School stayed independent in 1945 although the King's High School For Girls was not fully independent till 1976.

The Funding of the 1875 Scheme

Most of the Charities of Warwick, especially those connected with education, contributed to the scheme of 1875 and a large contribution came from the Charity of King Henry VIII.

King Henry VIII's Charity gave 12 acres of land along the Myton Road on which to build the new premises for the Grammar School. It also gave the old College buildings (later scandalously sold for demolition) and an annual grant of around £460.

A massive contribution of £25,000 Consols came from the accumulation of income from Sir Thomas White's Charity and every five years a further sum of around £1,900 was paid.

The Charities of Earl Brooke, Matthew Busby, Richard Edgeworth, Sarah Greville, Robert Heath, Fulke Weale (both) and Sir Thomas Wheatley were absorbed within the scheme and annual grants were received from Richard Griffin's and Thomas Oken's Charity besides King Henry VIII's Estate. In 1877 Ann Johnson's Charity gave Landor House, its large garden and the adjoining cottages, plus an annuity of £50 per annum. In 1907 this annuity was replaced by a transfer of investments.

In 1898 the income from the Charities of Jane Tomkys and William Vyner were incorporated in the scheme and in 1908 Thomas Oken's Charity was forced to sell off properties so that investments of £8,000 already promised could be transferred to the scheme. In retrospect, E.G. Tibbits and others have pointed out that this meant that around half the income of Oken's Charity was thus transferred to the King's Schools Scheme, when around one sixth would have been a fairer figure – bearing in mind that originally only one sixth of the total Charity bequests involved education.

An indirect result of the scheme was that King Henry VIII's Charity sold property in 1877 so that the money could be invested in Consols. Several other Charities (for example Ann Johnson's) also did this and with hindsight, considering the upheavals and inflation of the twentieth century, this proved to be a poor business move.

There were many critics of the scheme of 1875 and undeniably the poor were robbed because a number of Charities which had given them support in times of hardship were incorporated in the schools scheme. In 1875 some caring Trustees of the Charities for the poor only voted to support the scheme because they felt that the only way to improve the lot of the poor was to offer poor children the chance of a good education by means of the few free scholarships at each of the King's schools which were available to clever pupils from the town. Also some middle class idealists in the later 19th century felt it was wrong to give doles of bread or money to poor people because it encouraged them to be dependent on handouts.

Later Headmasters

1876-1880 Rev. W.F. Macmichael
1880-1885 Rev. William Grundy
1885-1896 Rev. J. Pearce Way
1896-1902 Rev. Robert P. Browne
1902-1906 Rev. William T. Keeling
1906-1928 Mr H. S. Pyne (previously King's Middle School headmaster and the first H/M not to be clergyman). Died 1950 aged 86.
1928-1933 Mr G.A. Riding (left to become Headmaster of Aldenham School). Died 1982 aged 93.
1933-1936 Mr E. Percival Smith (left to be Headmaster of Bradford Grammar School).
1936-1962 Mr A.H.B. Bishop (Retired to Bladon, Oxfordshire). Died 1969.
1962-1977 Mr P. W. Martin (Retired and now living in Kenilworth).
1977-1988 Mr J.A. Strover (Retired and now living in Suffolk).

Wonderful Margin Notes

As to a lively description of what Warwick School was like in the later 19th century, an annotated copy of "The History of Warwick School" by Leach, provided many wonderful comments. This copy of the book appeared to have been purchased by Warwick Library after the death of the Old Warwickian and I became utterly fascinated by the remarks, carefully written in pencil on many of the pages. I offer a selection of these comments to convey the spirit of life at Warwick School from around 1880 to 1895

Next to the photograph of headmaster William Grundy were the emotive words *"A flogger!"* which comment surely needs no elaboration.

The Old Warwickian had the highest praise for Dr Way. On one page was written,

"The finest H.M. the school ever had – and a gentleman in every sense of the word – firm, just and kind, with a sense of humour ... I liked him very much as a boy ... He made Warwick School and brought the right atmosphere with him to make it a really good public school.

Dr Way had his favourites, myself among them, but caned them just the same – possibly more severely when they deserved it. I had it once for taking eggs from a sitting pheasant in Lord Warwick's Park!

Dr Way hated the new pronunciation of Latin which had started to creep in and on a Speech Day he ridiculed it by giving an example of the sublime to the ridiculous which under the new idea turned the majestic words 'Veni, vidi, vici' into 'weny, weedy, weeky!'

Dr Way's young wife (he had been a bachelor when he came to Warwick) was obviously idolised by many of the boys. Our "scribbler" had commented about her—

"Known as Gerty – she was considerably younger than JPW and had a lisp and was quite nice … After hall there was quite a competition as to which boy held the door open for her and Dr Way as they returned to their house."

There were some descriptive remarks concerning the teachers at Warwick School in the time of Dr Way. Concerning Robert Davies he had said *"Had a good heart under a rugged and rather surly manner. Known as Bear Davies – I liked him"*. Of John Wishart Liddell he wrote,

"Son of a wine merchant and rather flashy in his dress when off duty. Florid with a black moustache which contrary to tradition (apart from Army Sgt Majors) he waxed … His favourite expresssion when trouncing a boy for bad work in class was 'You double distilled essence of donkey dom' in which one may trace something of the wine merchant's vocabulary." The French and German master Herr Ulrich was described as *"A nice old thing who punished bad behaviour in class by giving the culprit 50 French verbs to write out which on any argument rose rapidly from 50 to 500 – reduced to about 10 when class ended."*

Some of my favourite comments concerned the Cadet Force. Our writer had commented in a margin

"Our service rifles were Martini – Henry. Kick you into a ditch but would stop anything. I missed getting my marksmanship at Stratford on Avon by one mark."

However my favourite comment of all was that which described Mr J.W.Forbes taking command of the Cadet Corps in 1894. If some of the boarders have ever felt that the playing field was haunted, perhaps this will explain why.

"When Forbes was appointed to officer the Corps, he used to go out on the playing field by moonlight to get used to his sword and practise saluting with it. We boys could see it flashing in the moonlight from the dormitory windows."

THE TWENTIETH CENTURY

Headmasters from 1906 to 1962

Horace Seymour Pyne, a graduate of Trinity College Dublin, was the first headmaster of Warwick School to be a scientist and not a clergyman. Appointed as the Headmaster of the King's Middle School in 1898 he took charge of the combined school when amalgamation with Warwick School came about in 1906. He was interested in all the latest inventions, especially those which concerned photography, magic lanterns and gramophones and he succeeded in giving the school the stability it had lacked for so long. His own three sons attended Warwick School but sadly three of his five children died young, including Eric, the youngest who was killed during the First World War.

Although he was only headmaster for 5 years from 1928 to 1933, Mr Riding

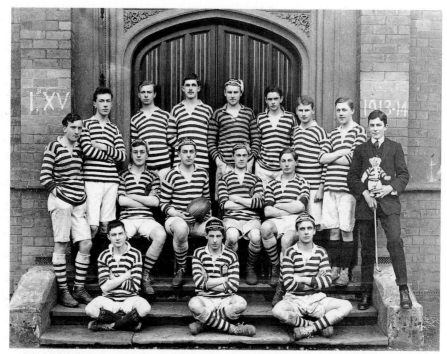

SADLY FIVE MEMBERS OF THIS RUGBY XV OF 1913/14 AND THE TOUCH JUDGE WERE TO DIE IN THE FIRST WORLD WAR. The names of those who were killed are underlined. (left to right) (Back row) J.D. Franklin, R.J. Farmer, C.H. Bancroft, W.H. Miller, C.R.W. Lamplough, W.E. Davies V.A. Peers. (Middle row) G.W. Beeston-Bancroft, L.T.C. Seaman, C.G. Dixon (Capt.), H.J. Smith, A.H. Dawkes, R.B. Holcroft (Touch Judge), (Front row) H.E. Priday, E.W. Pyne (the Headmaster's son), E.L. Ward. (Warwick School Archives)

remained in touch with Warwick all his long life. A popular although strict man, Mr Riding presided over two notable happenings. Firstly in 1928 the poet John Masefield, an Old Boy of the school, distributed the prizes on Speech Day and in 1931 the school coat of arms was granted.

In 1936 Mr A.H.B. Bishop became headmaster and thus began a highly successful period in the school's history. Born in Cornwall, Mr Bishop had been an infantryman in the First World War. After the war he obtained a first class honours degree in Chemistry at Jesus College, Oxford and he took his M.A. Degree in 1926. Teaching posts prior to his arrival in Warwick included being a resident tutor at Westminster College in London, sixth form science master at Radley College and six years as headmaster of Magdalen College School, Brackley.

Said to be kind, but very firm with the boys, he was much respected at Warwick and in his time the number of pupils rose from 339 in 1936 to 742 in 1962. Mr

Bishop presided over some traumatic times in the school, not least maintaining the Independent status of the school when the 1944 Act forced many changes in education. Although not a sportsman himself, he never failed to walk around the school field on games afernoons and often sat in a favourite spot near the engineering shop to watch school cricket matches.

Besides being Headmaster, Mr Bishop was a Trustee of King Henry Vlll's Charity for many years.

ON 6TH NOVEMBER 1958 QUEEN ELIZABETH, THE QUEEN MOTHER VISITED WARWICK SCHOOL TO PERFORM THE OPENING CEREMONY OF THE NEW COMMEMORATIVE WROUGHT IRON MAIN GATES. Head boy Paul Ramage and the junior boys, caps in hand ready to give three hearty cheers for her majesty, stood on one side of the main doorway whilst some of the masters (Barry Young shown right) and their wives stood on the other. Beside her majesty walked the headmaster Mr A.H.B. Bishop and Alderman Guy Nelson can be seen behind. (BY)

Headmasters from 1962 to 1988

Appointed headmaster in 1962 at the age of 46, Patrick Martin soon became a most respected figure in Warwick. Like his predecessor he too was a Trustee of King Henry VIII's Charity for a number of years.

Having been born in Windermere and educated at Windermere Grammar School and Balliol College Oxford, during the Second World War he served (1940-46) as a G.S.O. in the Royal Artillery, amongst other places fighting in Burma with the 14th Army.

His first teaching post was at Abingdon School (1938-46) but after the war he became senior history master at Workington Grammar School (1946-49). After a spell as Assistant Education Officer for Brighton, he became headmaster of Chipping Norton Grammar School in 1952, leaving to become headmaster of Lincoln School in 1957. The 15 years in which Mr Martin was headmaster were very successful ones from the point of view of Warwick School and as a local J.P., lay reader and member of numerous committees, his public service won him many admirers. When he retired in 1977 he served for a while on Warwickshire County Council and he wrote "A History of Heart of England Building Society" which was published in 1981.

Recently I was privileged to visit Mr Martin at his home in Kenilworth and we discussed many aspects of the history of Warwick School.

WARWICK SCHOOL PREFECTS IN 1970-71. From left to right (front row) J.P.W. Long, I.J. Beeching (Second Master), P.W. Martin (Headmaster), B.D. Joseph, (Second row) J. Aulich, J. Wilde, G.E. Neath, W.H. Askew, R.C. Barnwell, J.M. Collins, (Third row) C.H. Whomersley, T.J. Reeve, K.G. Tallett, P.N. Hawker, M.F. Hancock, (Back row) A.C. Shaw, S.A. Thorpe Smith. (Warwick School Archives)

"Warwick School in the twentieth century has been essentially a day school with a minority of boarders. It follows that the needs of the day boys were paramount, but the existence of the boarding house served a very real need," he explained.

As regards the topical question of co-education Mr Martin said that from his experience, having taught in both single-sex and mixed schools,

"Whilst mixed secondary schools are good from a social point of view, often a high academic price is paid for the privilege. Generally boys needed to be pressurised more than girls and it is difficult to apply the right amount of pressure in a mixed school".

With the media reporting high success rates for single sex schools in the examination tables of 1993 and 1994, it would appear that many parents would agree with him that single sex schools are the best choice for many able pupils.

I was most interested to learn that when Mr Martin began his career at Abingdon School, the headmaster was then William Grundy who was the son of the former headmaster of Warwick School. The younger William who had been born in Warwick looked very much like his father who had been headmaster from 1880 to 1885.

John Strover, a 46 year old Mathematics graduate of Trinity College Oxford, succeeded Mr Martin when he retired in 1977. Previously assistant master at Canford School (1955 -58) Mr Strover had been assistant master and careers master at Harrow School from 1958 to 1970 and headmaster of Kingston Grammar School from 1970 to 1977. He presided over a period of transition at Warwick and during his time various new buildings were added. Also £200,000 was successfully raised to "top up" a Bursary Fund, following the withdrawal of scholarships funded by the County Council in 1978.

Mr Strover left Warwick on his retirement in 1988 when Dr Philip Cheshire the present headmaster was appointed.

Some Other Notable Members of Staff

Perhaps it is unfair to single out certain members of staff, whilst omitting to mention others perhaps equally worthy or longserving, but the following pen-portraits of certain characters will surely strike a chord with many ex-pupils. These people must represent all the excellent staff who have taught at Warwick School during the twentieth century.

In 1899 Marmaduke Musson Clark had been appointed to the staff of the King's Middle School and when the school merged with Warwick School in 1906 he moved with it. "Nobby" was said to be rather like the fictional "Mr Chips" and although he was well past retiring age, he was asked to continue teaching throughout the Second World War. A particularly capable teacher, he became Bursar and later second master. After 1946 he became honorary bursar and he remained at Warwick until he had completed 50 years of service in 1949. He was the honorary secretary of the O.W. club and his efforts helped to raise the required sum for the Memorial Fund after the war.

THE RT. HON. J. ENOCH POWELL, M.B.E. MP TALKS WITH HEAD BOY STEPHEN LOVEGROVE AND DEPUTY JOHN FLYNN AFTER WARWICK SCHOOL SPEECH-DAY IN OCTOBER 1984. In his speech Mr Powell made an eloquent plea for the teaching of Latin and Greek to continue. (Photograph courtesy of Leamington Spa Courier).

Marmaduke Clark died in 1955 aged 79 and The Portcullis Magazine spoke of his great strength "physical, mental and moral". Said to be proud of his Scottish ancestry, he was in many ways a charismatic figure and his unusual hobby of woodcutting was quite in character. When he died, his funeral took place at St Nicholas Church and the entire upper school attended with the headmaster Mr Bishop reading the lesson.

For over 44 years Lt-Col. P.N.G. Whitlam, O.B.E. was associated with Warwick School and over the years he performed a variety of roles including laboratory assistant, curator and Cadet Corps commander.

He arrived in 1920 after his career at London University had been cut short by war service in the Royal Flying Corps. As he was so efficient as a laboratory assistant and quickly became indispensable whenever practical problems arose anywhere around the school, the post of curator was created for him. During the Second World War his contribution was particulary valuable and in 1942 he took over command of the C.C.F. He was a director of air-raid precautions and he engaged in secret work for the Government.

COL. P.N.G.
WHITLAM BEING
PRESENTED WITH
HIS T.D. AWARD
AT WARWICK
SCHOOL IN 1951.
(Warwick School
Archives)

In 1951 he was promoted to Lt-Col. awarded the T.D. and then in 1955 came the O.B.E. As he lived in Senior House he was able to give the boarders much practical help and he became a friend to many.

In 1963 he relinquished the command of the Cadet Corps and in 1965 he officially retired from his other duties. His retirement home was at New Milton, Hampshire, where he died in March 1984.

Few people have done more for Warwick School than J.M.A. Marshall who has been directly associated as pupil and teacher for over 37 years. He entered as a pupil in the Upper Fourth in 1930 and left in 1935 as Captain of School, Captain of Cricket, Captain of Fives and a member of the First XV. After training at St Paul's College and beginning a teaching career, he did war service in the Physical Training Corps and later the Royal Artillery, rising to the rank of Lt-Col. during his service mainly in the Middle East.

Jack Marshall returned to Warwick School in 1946 to teach games and the third form but he was soon promoted to be Head of the Junior School. Besides his teaching, he also carried on a career in first class cricket and in all he played 28 matches for Warwickshire between 1946 and 1950. An all rounder, his best bowling performance for Warwickshire was 5 -65 in his debut match in 1946. He also captained Leamington Cricket Club from 1955 to 1963 and since 1966 he has been Club President. After his playing days were over he took on a prominent role in local and county cricket administration.

Following retirement in 1978, Jack still lives in Leamington and he is much concerned with the O.W. club.

With a degree in Mathematics from Merton College Oxford, R.H. Thornton first came to the Mathematics Department in 1948. He was an enthusiastic teacher and his love of rugby football ensured that together with Jack Marshall and Ken Freeborn he helped coach the Senior XXX for many years. In 1963 he took over as Head of the Mathematics Department and this he continued for 20 years. From 1980 he became second master and his great energy and kindness won him many friends.

Since his retirement in 1989, Ralph Thornton has been very active, amongst other things assisting in various capacities at St Mary's Church. Besides being a Trustee of Oken's Charity (Chairman from 1990 to 1993) he is connected with many other aspects of life in Warwick.

Two of the four members of staff already described were second masters at some time during their time at Warwick, but there were several other second masters who must be mentioned.

Robert Mitchell (1938-1939 and 1945 -53) did much for the school and some years after he left he became the first headmaster of Kenilworth Grammar School. Felix Dugdale (1938-1964) for many years the Head of Modern Languages, was second master from 1954 until his retirement in 1964 and John Beeching, Head of Science from 1954-70 was second master from 1970 to his retirement in 1980.

Governors

Always vital to the well-being of a successful school, the King's (Warwick) Schools Foundation seems to have been fortunate in that a succession of conscientious Governors have been running affairs since 1875. Not that they always made the correct decisions; some blunders were made such as the refusal to fund a new boarding house in 1888. When Dr Way left Warwick, the Governors had to pay out £3500 to buy the Junior boarding house which he had funded personally whilst Headmaster. Also when the Middle and Grammar School amalgamated, instead of offering the Middle School buildings to the Girls' School, they were sold to St Mary's Church and the Girls' School had to rent sections of the buildings for the next 64 years.

In 1906 the Governors were nominated by different groups. Warwick Town Council nominated 5 Governors, Leamington Town Council 2, King Henry VIII's Charity 4, United Charities 2 and Oken's Charity and Oxford University 1 each. There were also several ex-officio Governors such as The Earl of Warwick, the Marquis of Hertford and the Mayor of Warwick. Some of the Governors were outstanding people – those who had a tremendous influence on the schools and the town of Warwick.

Sir Michael Lakin

Although he died over sixty years ago, the name of Sir Michael Lakin is still remembered today and he was one of the most famous and hard-working Warwick Schools' Governors of all time. Also he was for many years a Trustee of King Henry Vlll's and other local charities.

Born in Malvern in 1846 he came to Warwick in 1870 and for many years was connected with the family firm of Greaves, Bull and Lakin, cement manufacturers who owned Harbury Cement Works.

In 1884 he was appointed to represent the Trustees of King Henry Vlll's Charity on the Governing Body of Warwick School and in 1888 he became a Manager of the girls' school. For some years he was Deputy Chairman of the Governors of Warwick School and from 1925 he was Chairman of the Govenors of the girls' school. It is said that in six years he did not miss a single committee meeting.

In 1889 he had been elected an original member of the County Council and in 1899 he was High Sheriff of Warwickshire. Having been elected to Warwick Town Council in 1901, from 1902 to 1905 he was Mayor of Warwick. In 1905 he was granted the Freedom of Warwick, the first time this honour had been given, and in 1909 he was created a Baronet.

Even a London Museum remembers his name for in 1898 the bones of a large ichthyosauros, measuring 19 feet 4 inches were found in the Stockton quarry owned by his company. These remains he generously gave to the British Museum and Warwick Museum also was given interesting prehistoric relics.

Politically a Liberal, he became the Vice Chairman of the County Council in 1929 and when he died in March 1931 aged 84, he was mourned by many. He was interred in Bishops' Itchington churchyard in a private ceremony, but a large memorial service in St Mary's Church Warwick was attended by hundreds of people including the Trustees of King Henry Vlll's Charity and the head teachers of the King's Schools. Mr G.A. Riding, headmaster of Warwick School said of him, "*He stands for me as a perfect example of the old-world English Christian gentleman.*"

The Buildings of Warwick School

In 1879 the present buildings of the school were completed on land donated by the Trustees of the Charity of King Henry VIII. Designed by J. Cundall, the architect who designed Leamington Town Hall, the imposing mock Tudor buildings were opened on 1st August 1879.

It was not long before additions were made and the following is a summary of some of the developments since 1879.

1884   Workshop
1886   Cricket pavilion
1887   Avenue of lime trees to celebrate Queen Victoria's Jubilee
1888   New Junior boarding house built by Dr Way
1890   Gymnasium

1893-5 Further extensions to Chapel (chancel etc)

1905/6 New Science Block

1907   Pit for swimming bath begun, but unfinished till 1912.

1910   School changed from gas to electricity lighting.

1919   Chapel Gallery begun in memory of those who died in the Great War.

1925   Sports Field extended. New pavilion after fire destroys old one.

1926   Big School – refurbishment.

1957   New Gymnasium

1957   New Science Block (enlarged 1965 and 1974)

1969   Guy Nelson Hall
        Big School refurbished as Library

1972   New Dining Hall and Squash Courts

1974/5 Old "New Buildings" demolished. New Science Rooms/Mathematics Rooms/Drawing Office Extension.

1979   Second storey of new building – 6 classrooms/bookstore
        Sixth Form Centre

1982   New Economics Block

BIG SCHOOL IN 1902. Looking towards the north, this shows the room before the gallery was built at the North end and the stage extension at the South end. There are various Honours Boards on the walls and the room was lit by multiple gas lights. (RHT)

A SIMILAR VIEW OF BIG SCHOOL ABOUT 75 YEARS LATER IN THE 1970s.
Having been adapted for use as a Library, the room was also used for lessons. This
photograph also provides a nostalgic glimpse of leather satchels. (BY)

1986   New Mathematics Block & Computer Room

1987   Design Centre

1988   Extension to Science Block

1989   Main entrance of school refurbished.

1990   New Classics Block

1991   Old swimming pool filled in – indoor pool opened. New Science and
Technology Laboratory in Junior School

1994   Sports Hall

Old Warwickians and Personal Memories

Formed in 1895, for over a century the O.W. club has helped to keep former
pupils and staff in touch with Warwick School. Each year a new President is elected
and by means of this tradition some eminent and loyal Old Warwickians have been
honoured.

Over the years there have been many locally famous and some internationally
famous men who were formerly pupils at Warwick School. An interesting character

OLD WARWICKIAN JOHN MASEFIELD 1878-1967. POET LAUREATE 1930-1967. Perhaps the most famous old Warwickian of all, John Masefield was a boarder at Warwick from 1888 to 1891. Born in Ledbury, orphan Masefield was only 10 when sent to Warwick, but disliking boarding-school, he left to go to sea, beginning the adventures which gave him material for many poems and novels. In 1928 he returned to Warwick School to present the prizes at Speech Day. (By courtesy of the National Portrait Gallery, London)

who attended the school in the 1840s was Sabine Baring-Gould, a Devonshire rector who was a novelist, antiquarian and expert on West Country folklore. He wrote numerous literary works including the famous hymn "Onward Christian Soldiers". Both Richard Child Heath and Sidney Flavel Junior attended in the time of Herbert Hill and John Masefield (1888-1891) Poet Laureate from 1930 to 1967 is perhaps the most famous of all but Sir George Catlin (1906-1913)a professor and political writer was also internationally recognised. He was the husband of writer Vera Brittain and father of politician Shirley Williams, and being a local man he was buried in Old Milverton churchyard when he died in 1979.

Harry Greenway (1946-53) has been the conservative M.P. for Ealing North since 1979 and in 1983 he was the President of the O.W.

Dennis Freeman (1923-28) was Town Clerk of Warwick for many years, often being nicknamed "Mr Warwick" before his death in 1981 aged 68. Famous pianists Denis Matthews (1932-6) and Eric Hope (1928-31) will be remembered by many as will Phil Bromley (1942-47) a cricketer who played 49 matches for Warwickshire between 1947 -56. Arthur Godfrey Brown, a pupil in the early 1930s, won two medals in the Olympic Games in Berlin in 1936 – a silver medal in the 400m with a time of 46.7 and a gold medal in the 4 x 400m relay. Later he became headmaster of the Royal Grammar School Worcester.

However, the most illustrious O.W. still alive is probably Lord Mulley (1929-36) whose life story I find absolutely fascinating.

As a boy, Fred Mulley lived in Clemens Street and in Leamington attended Bath Place School. His parents were far from being well-off and at the age of eleven talented Fred was offered a County scholarship by both the Leamington College and Warwick School. He had actually started at Leamington College (as the term began first) when he was tempted away by Warwick headmaster Mr Riding.

During his time at Warwick School, apart from being a prefect in his final year, he won numerous essay prizes and was Chairman of the League of Nations Union and Captain of the School Chess Team from 1934-6. However he was not only an academic, he also captained the Second XV, was Captain of Tudor House from 1935-6, captained the House Fives and was a Sgt. in the O.T.C. winning his Cert. A in 1934.

Fred Mulley left school in 1936 and for several years he worked in a local Health Office. During the Second World War, after service with the Royal Worcester Regiment, he was captured in France in 1940 and remained a POW (spending time studying when possible) until 1945. Following liberation, he went to Christ Church, Oxford where he gained a first class degree in Philosophy, Politics and Economics and he was then offered a Fellowship at St Catharine's College, Cambridge. In 1950 he entered Parliament when he was elected Labour M.P. for the Park Division of Sheffield and he represented that constituency for the next 33 years. His great ability was soon recognised and he held various ministerial posts in Harold Wilson's and James Callaghan's governments including Aviation, Disarmament, Transport, and Education & Science. Having left the Commons the previous year, he was created a life peer, Baron Mulley of Manor Park in Sheffield, in 1984 and since that time he has been active in the House of Lords, attending debates wherever possible.

In December 1993 I was privileged to visit Lord Mulley at the House of Lords, where we had tea together and talked of his career. Modestly and with humour he answered my queries and explained that in the House of Lords there was generally a higher standard of debate than in the Commons for individual Lords only chose to speak if they had specialist knowledge of a subject and none needed to impress any constituents. For 11 years from 1958 to 1969 Fred Mulley sponsored the O.W's London Dinner at the House of Commons and in 1969 he was O.W. President.

Having described to me how in 1940 a bullet had clipped his ear after hitting a buckle in his helmet, Lord Mulley smiled as he said *"I've had a lucky and enjoyable life"* and I believe Warwick School should be proud of its famous son.

Personal Memories

Perhaps the best way to end this chapter is with a selection of quotations from various ex-staff and pupils who can summarise far better than I ever can what life at Warwick School was really like in the twentieth century.

"The school was much smaller then, in 1949, so for Assembly the whole school could get into Big School (what is now the Library). The Library then was where the secretary's office is now and for lunches in the dining room (the panelled part before the extension) everyone had his own place and we began and ended with a formal Latin grace. When you came to school in the morning and went to chapel, you lined both sides of the corridor between the headmaster's study and the cloisters and the headmaster, with cap and gown, would process between the lines, inspecting his troops, telling one boy off for dirty shoes, another for long hair ...Everyone wore caps and when you saw a member of staff in the sreet or any adult you knew, you were not just expected to touch your caps, you were instructed to take them off so that the name on the label inside could be seen."

From his speech to the boys on his retirement by B.W. Young (Classics teacher and house master 1949 -1985)

"In those days, prefects were allowed to beat boys ...we had to bend over in the prefect's study and be whacked on the backside with a gym shoe. The trick of course was to pad the rear quarters with lots of borrowed pairs of gym shorts.

My most memorable game for the school XI was my first – played at Edgbaston against King Edward's School, Birmingham. I was lucky enough to capture two wickets and only in later years did the significance of the two captures dawn on me – they were none other than O.S. Wheatley (the Ossie Wheatley who went on to play for Warwickshire and captain Glamorgan) and A.C. Smith who went on to play for Warwickshire. He still holds one test batting record and is now the Chief

Executive of the Test and County Cricket Board. Warwick School went on to win the match, played in May 1953, by six wickets."
From John Yarwood (1947-53) now a well-known sports columnist and media cricket commentator in Western Australia.

"I used to train and organize the Warwick School swimming team that performed in the 25m open-air swimming pool. ... The horrified expressions on the faces of the visiting teams as they turned past the gymsasium and were hit by the keen sou'westerly breeze that blew relentlessly from the Banbury Road across the playing fields rippling the pool water, are long remembered."
Ken Freeborn Head of P.E. 1957-1992 (who is himself remembered by many for being able to walk round that old swimming pool on his hands and climb ropes without using his legs)

"Rugger was a serious matter."
Arthur Measures of Mill Street (1921-28) when asked if he could recall any amusing incidents about his time in the school XV.

THE KING'S HIGH SCHOOL FOR GIRLS AND WARWICK PREPARATORY SCHOOL

Not until both the boys' schools had been rehoused could the girls' school, planned under the scheme of 1875, be brought into being. Once the Middle School had vacated Landor House in 1878, various conversions were carried out and in the Spring of 1879 twenty two girls were finally able to start. Landor House, the adjacent cottages and the large garden, in which new premises had been built for the King's Middle School, had been given to the King's Schools Foundation by the Trustees of Ann Johnson's Charity (largely set up to benefit the poor) in lieu of £100 annually which the Charity had promised.

1879-1922 Well Begun

Right from the start the school was a success, possibly because the first headmistress Mary Fisher seemed determined to succeed. Life was often difficult for the young 22 year old from West Ham, who had previously been an assistant mistress at West Ham High School For Girls, but she provided her new school with flair and stability.

Her sound judgement and common sense won her much respect in Warwick and it was sad that recurring health problems, possibly caused by the enormous stress and financial restraints she worked under, eventually caused her retirement in 1895.

"*She was a pioneer and had to prove to the world that girls had brains and intellects and could pass examinations.*" So said Miss Lloyd Evans at the Jubilee Celebration of King's High School in 1929.

Although she left the district in 1895, Miss Fisher (Mrs Kelson) continued to keep in touch with the school, being one of the Vice-Presidents of the Old Girls' Association for many years.

Miss Margaret Lea (Mrs Gardner) took over as headmistress in 1896. A former pupil of Manchester Girls' High School, she studied mathematics at Girton College, Cambridge where she proved a brilliant student.

Impeccably dressed in either tailored dresses or satin afternoon gowns, with long copper coloured hair she was a memorable figure. In those times it was impossible for women to continue teaching after marriage and it must have surprised no one when this beautiful and talented woman left to marry.

In those early years of the twentieth century many changes were going on in education and from 1902 there had been scholarships to the school paid for by the

County. Being the counterpart of the Boys' Middle School (renamed King's County School in 1905) King's High School likewise was receiving various grants from the County Council.

A kind and deeply religious person, Ella Mary Edgehill was appointed headmistress in 1913 and she faced a number of pressing problems. It was clear that the school had insufficient income from the King's Schools Foundation for salaries and the school could only afford to employ teachers fresh from college. The County Council was asked to help and more money was made available via a special County Rate. By 1914 the school enjoyed a fine reputation and had 245 pupils and by 1920 this number had risen to 361.

The First World War was a particularly difficult time and in Morning Assembly each day Miss Edgehill would pray for the victims of the slaughter at the Front and their loved ones, and read messages of hope from the bible. When fathers, brothers and friends were being killed or horrifically injured in France and elsewhere, with few telephones and no regular radio or television broadcasts, it often took days for any news to be received. Many women wished there was more they could do and at King's High School and elsewhere food parcels were prepared and sent to the troops at the Front. Miss Montifiore (1901-1917) the senior French mistress and later second mistress, who rented the old Middle School headmaster's house in The Butts after the Middle School had amalgamated with the Grammar School in 1906, organised sewing parties of sixth formers at her house to help the war effort and the

I NEVER REALLY APPRECIATED HOW TALL MISS DOORLY WAS UNTIL I SAW THIS SNAP, TAKEN IN THE PLAYGROUND IN JULY 1929. (From the left) Miss Watkin, Miss Roberts, Miss Pettle, Miss Doorly (Headmistress), Miss Sharp, Miss Hutchinson, and Miss Wheeler-Robinson are shown here. (King's High School Archives)

sixth form also did other war work such as copying out in triplicate certain statistics for the War Office.

In 1921 Miss Edgehill resigned and the reign of her successor Miss Gardner (Lady Moberley) as headmistress was very short as she chose to marry within a year of her appointment and therefore resigned. Although she was only headmistress for a short time, Lady Moberley always kept in touch with the school until her death in 1975 at the age of 83. In 1954, when the 75th anniversary of the school occurred, she presented the prizes at Speech Day held in the Warwick Cinema.

1922-1944 Miss Doorly

In appointing the dynamic Victoria Eleanor Louise Doorly as headmistress in 1922 the Governors perhaps made their wisest decision ever, for innovations begun by Miss Doorly are still continued over 60 years later. Although she was headmistress during the difficult years of the depression, in her time the school went from strength to strength and enjoyed a fine reputation in many fields.

IN 1937 PRINCESS ALICE OF ATHLONE PRESENTED THE PRIZES AT KING'S HIGH SCHOOL SPEECH DAY, HELD IN THE COUNTY CINEMA. The platform party included Councillor Guy Nelson, Mayor of Warwick; Marjorie, Countess of Warwick; Mrs Lloyd Evans O.B.E.; Mrs E.L. Tibbits and Mrs Pitman. A red carpet was laid for the princess outside Landor House and in 1938 pupil Joan Salisbury recalled, "We had to practise curtseying and walking backwards on the school hall stage and Miss Bate had to be ready to catch us if we fell." I saw octogenarian Miss Bate recently and she well remembered those elaborate precautions! (King's High School Archives)

Born in 1880 and having been educated at Leamington High School (now Kingsley) and in France, Miss Doorly possessed a B.A. in Modern Languages and an M.A. Degree in History, both from London University. Her first book "England in Her Days of Peace" had been published in 1920 and she counted various writers and poets, in particular Walter De La Mare, amongst her friends. She had taught at the pioneering North London Collegiate School and had been headmistress of Twickenham County School prior to coming to Warwick.

At first her modern ideas must have seemed outrageous to some in Warwick, but her enormous ability and sound judgement soon made her popular with parents. However many day girls, who never saw her in relaxed mood, always seemed to be in awe of her. She seemed to possess a strange mixture of Victorian prudery, which made her abhor make-up even on a resident domestic assistant on her day off, and an aesthetic love of beauty, which made her enthuse over the finest music, poetry and art. Perhaps her greatest triumph was to set up the system of school and form councils which is still in modified use today, having served to introduce several generations of girls to democratic government.

GENERALLY RECOGNISED AS FORMING ONE OF THE FINEST VIEWS IN WARWICK, EASTGATE, LANDOR HOUSE AND THE COTTAGES HAVE CHANGED LITTLE SINCE 1788. In that year Eastgate was "recased in stone" by Francis Hiorne at the expense of King Henry VIII's Charity which then owned the building. The King's High School has occupied Landor House (reconstructed 1693) and the cottages (built c1482) since 1879 and they have leased Eastgate since 1916. This photograph was taken in the 1950s when Miss Bate's car was often to be seen outside the cottages. (Photograph courtesy of Leamington Spa Courier)

The Visit of Professor Salvemini

Always a person to offer someone a fair hearing, Miss Doorly caused some eyebrows to be raised on 22nd March 1926 when she allowed Professor Gaetano Salvemini, the distinguished Italian historian who had been forced to flee Italy by the dictator Mussolini, to give an address in the school hall. The meeting was chaired by Bolton King, the Director of Education for Warwickshire and in the audience were senior pupils, besides numerous adult visitors.

Margaret Thomas (nee Stiles) then a senior pupil and now aged 85, said that she had never forgotten Salvemini's visit. It had made a great impression on her and on many other pupils.

However Miss Doorly was later informed by the Chairman of the Governors that many people were displeased with her for having Salvemini in the school and to have so controversial a figure to speak to senior pupils in 1926 was indeed a very daring move.

Miss Doorly always had the courage of her convictions and was not afraid to speak her mind, thus giving the kind of clear leadership which is so often lacking in modern society.

The Last Years of Miss Doorly's Period as Headmistress

The years from 1938 to 1944 when Miss Doorly retired at the end of the Christmas term, were particularly eventful from many points of view. On a personal level this time was very successful for her for during the 1930s she had written several children's books which had proved to be best sellers and which were republished as some of the earliest paperbacks for children.

During the war Miss Doorly did all she could to help the war effort and keep her pupils informed of the news. Well travelled and with an excellent knowledge of many languages, including Norwegian, she herself acted as a translator for the Government and the school adopted three merchant ships, giving much support to the crews.

One extremely sad occurrence in 1943 which some ex-pupils still remember vividly, was the death of the popular Miss Margaret Watkin in a road accident as she cycled to school along the Rugby Road in Leamington. The 61 year old teacher had taught Geography at King's High for over 30 years and her death gave all the pupils a great sense of shock. Her funeral, held in Spencer Street Church, Leamington, was attended by Councillor Ansell, Mayor of Warwick, together with Miss Doorly and many of the staff and pupils including Head Girl Sheila Spencer.

The 64 year old Eleanor Doorly eventually retired at Christmas 1944 and she went to live in Dartmouth, writing another book about France before she died in 1950 aged 70.

Miss Doorly By Those Who Knew Her

In a previous book I devoted a chapter to Miss Doorly. Following publication I received scores of letters, almost all of them describing memories of "Aunt Do" or her Alsatian Vlah. I offer a selection of quotations from these letters in order to bring Miss Doorly to life in a way I never could.

"Miss Doorly was a remarkable person with advanced ideas."
   Eileen Barret (Marshall 1917-1924)

"Miss Doorly was not particularly liked as she had some strange ideas. We didn't know she had written books! She stopped Girl Guides as she didn't approve of them. … I think Aunt Do only noticed girls who stood out as being anti-authority. … Vlah used to go round to lessons given by Aunt Do. Alsatians were new to England and many people were afraid of them. As a prefect I used to go to the study occasionally and Vlah used to stand and put his paws on my shoulders."
   Cicely Elliot (Cooke 1919-1927)

"I was fortunate in being offered a large attic room in Landor House, which then accommodated about 30 boarders. In this way I shared in a very happy community life.
   Another endearing quality was her love of horses and riding. She owned a spirited pony Tara and persuaded me to take a course of riding lessons after which we would often set out along the Fosse Way or elsewhere, with Tara and a bicycle, and take turns in riding each of them!"
   Mrs Nash-Williams, now aged 95. As Miss Luck she taught classics at KHS from 1922-1928.

"I well remember Miss Doorly: I was a bit scared of her and absolutely terrified of Vlah. To this day I steer very clear of Alsatians."
   Dorothy Williams (1924-1925)

"I recall one sensational night when it was alleged that a senior in Cottage Dorm had seen the Ghost … down swooped Doorly in her faded blue dressing gown, quilted but elderly, her grey plait bouncing on her shoulder, with a huge bottle of syrup of figs and a large serving spoon in her hand. Everyone had a dose, irrespective of whether they had seen the ghost or not. It was very chastening.
   I remember her commanding height and humorous lopsided smile and wonderful facility to raise a child's consciousness above the mundane thoughts of everyday."
   Eirwen Harbottle (Jones – Boarder 1932-1938)

"If my education under Miss Doorly did nothing else for me, it made me think for myself… When we went for our Russian or R.E. lessons, we would find Miss Doorly in her exquisitely furnished study, finishing her cigarette and glass of port."
   Beryl Darkes (Styles 1939-45)

"Those two remarkable teachers, Miss Naish and Miss Lord, taught me maths and then taught how to teach! ... Miss Doorly was a truly remarkable woman – she had a wonderful and provoking mind."
    Betty Rider (Helena Horler Pupil 1924-1930, Staff 1933 -38)

"Our assembled shuffles and coughs would die away to a waiting silence. Then Miss Doorly with her slight eclectic bend came down the side of the big hall. She was tall and had this elegant remoteness – a kind of Olympian altitude. She always wore a purple (or a blue) hand-woven suit with drooping coat top and decorative edging; and a pure, spotless, creaseless white silk blouse; essences of perfection never to be forgotten ... Her voice was low, with amused high lights that gave it colour. I can still hear it."
    Pamela Colebourn (1922-31)

"In 1924 I was Secretary of the Science Club and Miss Doorly encouraged me to scour the newspapers for news of Mallory and Irving who were lost near the summit of Everest and also of Colonel Fawcett who was lost in the Amazon area. We all became so interested in the news and it really made me appreciate newspapers."
    Mary Woodall (Stiles 1914-25)

"I enjoyed it all – even Aunt Do saying "Come and talk about yourself" which was her opening gambit when you were invited to her room."
    Margaret Thomas (Stiles 1915-28)

1945-7 Miss Wiseman (Mrs Gunn) and 1948-1970 Miss Hare

Miss Doorly retired at Christmas 1944 and Miss Wiseman was left to implement the 1944 Education Act with its far-reaching consequences.

Unlike Warwick School which opted to go Independent, King's High School was largely funded by the local Education Authority and the new Act required the closure of the Preparatory Department and also the boarding house. In order to save the Junior Department, Miss Smalley who had previously been in charge of it decided to form an independent Junior School, using the former rooms rented from St Mary's Church.

With 90 new pupils entering the Senior School via County scholarships each year, the premises were bursting at the seams and for the next few years every available room was used. The rooms in Landor House and the cottages which had previously only been used by the boarders had to be used as form rooms, likewise the rooms in Eastgate which had been sixth form library and staff rooms.

The vast number of girls who attended the school on a free place paid for by the local Education Authority did so whilst Miss Hare was headmistress, so she will be remembered by many. Having been born in Stamford in 1908 and educated at Stamford High School and Peterborough High School, she took a History degree at St Hugh's College, Oxford. Before coming to Warwick, she had held teaching posts at Barnsley, Ely, Newcastle-On-Tyne and Denbigh from 1932 to 1948

Miss Hare presided over a most difficult time in the school's history when following years of indecision, the Governors finally decided that the school was to go independent in April 1952. The County Council agreed to give 60 scholarships each year and 30 fee-payers formed the rest of each year's intake, this arrangement continuing after Direct Grant status was achieved in 1960. Desperately needed new buildings began to materialise in 1954 when Red Corridor was built, to be followed in 1960 by two new classrooms, 1963 the purchase of Red House, 1964 the building of Priory Annexe and 1967 when the new gymnasium and tunnel entrance to the playground was finished. When Miss Hare handed over to Miss Leahy in 1970, King's High School was firmly established as a Direct Grant school, able to attract many more fee payers than space permitted.

I must confess as a pupil I sometimes felt alienated by Miss Hare, but in retrospect I can see that in many ways her headship was good for the school.

Following her retirement in 1970, Frances Winifred Hare was elected to the County Council (1970-74), District Council (1973-76) and Warwick Town Council (1976-84). She died in 1989 aged 80 and Sigma, the last in a long line of her pet poodles , was allowed to remain in the Sherbourne Rest Home, run by ex-pupil Cherrie Chandley, where Miss Hare had ended her days.

1970-1987 Miss Leahy

Maureen Leahy is remembered as a most kind and conscientious person by many ex-pupils and staff and she presided over the difficult period when County Scholarships were gradually phased out and the entire school became fee-paying. I visited Miss Leahy recently at her home in Leamington and she spoke to me of her 17 years in charge of the school.

> *"We were a happy and united school, fortunate in our surroundings, with the staff working together.*
>
> *We were trying to help our pupils to be responsible. A strong self-governing element is really important and the School Council helped."*

Cheshire born, Miss Leahy had taken a Classics degree at London University before accepting teaching appointments at Manchester High School for Girls, King Edward VI Grammar School for Girls, Handsworth and being Headmistress of Christ's Hospital Girls' High School in Lincoln from 1964-70.

During Miss Leahy's time in Warwick, many other single-sex schools became co-educational but King's High School resisted any pressure to amalgamate with Warwick School. Miss Leahy had firm views on how the school should be run and she stuck to her principles.

There were drastic changes in education during the 1970s and the number of places financed by the County was reduced from 60 to 45 to 30 and finally withdrawn altogether. During the same period the Direct Grant status was being phased out, removing the Government subsidy. In those times the amount of money being paid to the Warwick Schools Foundation from King Henry Vlll's Charity was negligible and it says much for Miss Leahy and her staff that efficient

POPULAR ART TEACHER MRS SOREN IS SEEN HERE EXTOLLING THE VIRTUES OF VAN GOGH TO A GROUP OF UPPER THIRDS IN 1949. As Miss Struan Robertson, she joined the school in 1934, but left in 1942 to marry Baron Peter Soren, a Danish nobleman who had come to Britain to join the Air Force in the Second World War. Sadly he was killed and Scottish born Mrs Soren returned to teach Art at K.H.S. and she remained there until her untimely death in 1965. (King's High School Archives)

and economical management during the difficult years maintained the high academic standards for which the school had become renowned. Although there was a steady increase in the fees in Miss Leahy's time, the number of applications for places remained consistently high.

Being the last of the eight headmistresses to live in Landor House (the present headmistress lives nearby, although not in the school) Miss Leahy commented, *"It was a joy to live in Landor House"* and she laughed when I said how much I envied her in that respect.

The 200th anniversary of the poet Walter Savage Landor's birth in Landor House occurred in January 1975 and Miss Leahy described how a group of sixth-formers organised a small celebration, with readings from some of his better known works. Having studied the life and works of Walter and the Landor family as research for a previous book, I had grown particularly fond of this forgotten son of Warwick.

Other Notable Staff

K.H.S.W. has been particularly fortunate in having a succession of very able second mistresses over the years besides numerous other long-serving staff.

Second mistress and in charge of sixth form, Miss Ahrons (1897-1914) was a very talented woman. Although she left in 1914 to join the Board of Education in London as an inspector, she retained close ties with Warwick and came to speak at the Jubilee Celebrations in 1929.

Having joined the school to become second mistress shortly after Miss Doorly herself became headmistress, Edith Naish (1923-1958) had much to do with the running of the School Council. She and Miss Doorly worked extremely well

MISS MARGARET MARLOWE CONDUCTING A CELLO LESSON IN THE FRONT ATTIC OF LANDOR HOUSE IN 1960. From the start in 1879 the King's High School encouraged music lessons and people like Mr Warren, who taught violin for 40 years and began the school orchestra, and piano teachers such as O.G. the late Joan Bromwich, the late Phyllis Mason and Mrs Winifred German will be remembered by many. Although no longer connected with the school, Miss Marlowe and Mrs German are still very active in local musical circles. (King's High School Archives)

*SECOND MISTRESS JOAN
GREENWOOD PICTURED
SHORTLY BEFORE HER
RETIREMENT IN 1988. (JG)*

*MISS WHITTLESEY TEACHES AN ATTENTIVE CLASS IN THE
DEMONSTRATION ROOM IN 1960. Built in 1902 the "Dem" was capable of
squeezing numerous pupils onto its long, polished, tip-up seats and was hence used for
meetings of the School Council. In 1990 the Demonstration Room was dismantled, the old
desks and timbers being given to the Black Country Museum in Dudley which adapted some
parts of them for use in St James', a typical Victorian Primary School. (JG)*

together and the success of the school at that time must have depended a great deal on their efficient partnership. A fair-minded administrator and a gifted mathematician, Miss Naish retired in 1958. Although she went to live in Oxfordshire, she visited Warwick regularly until she died suddenly in July 1981 aged 89, having been active to her last day.

Dorothea Whittlesey joined the staff in 1938, having previously taught for 5 years at Uttoxeter Girls' School. Educated at King Edward's School, Birmingham and the Royal Holloway College, she had obtained a degree in Botany from London University. Miss Whittlesey became second mistress on the retirement of Miss Naish in 1958 and having inspired generations of pupils in her Botany and Biology lessons, was always pleased to see Old Girls. When she retired in July 1974, appropriately amongst her leaving gifts was a stainless steel spade from the pupils. Miss Whittlesey died in February 1992 at the age of 81, having suffered ill health for some years.

Joan Greenwood was appointed to the school in 1953, having previously spent 4 years teaching at Sibford Boarding School in Banbury. Her keen mathematical brain

OCTOBER 1978 SAW MISS HARE RETURN TO THE KING'S HIGH SCHOOL FOR SPEECH DAY WHEN THIS HISTORIC PHOTOGRAPH WAS TAKEN. From left to right they are Head Girl Fiona Barling, Deputy Head Girl Susan Hahn, Miss F. W. Hare (Headmistress from 1948 to 1970), Deputy Head Girl Kim Sweet and Miss M. Leahy (Headmistress). (JG)

soon made light of various administrative duties and her knowledge of various aspects of the school buildings became invaluable. Educated at Holme Valley Grammar School in Yorkshire , where she had been a contemporary of the late Roy Castle, and St Hilda's College Oxford where she obtained a degree in Mathematics, she later gained a Degree in Logic and Philosphy from London University. Previously third mistress, Miss Greenwood became Deputy headmistress on the retirement of Miss Whittlesey in 1974. and she continued until her retirement in 1988. Three headmistresses benefited from Miss Greenwood's organising ability and her great energy and common sense were much valued by staff and pupils alike.

Since then Miss Greenwood has led an active life, amongst other things tending the magnificent garden, with its wonderful camellias, which she and Miss Whittlesey planned together round their delightful home on the outskirts of Leamington Spa. In common with other ex-pupils, I am grateful for the help and advice which is still dispensed by this kind and sensible Yorkshire woman.

The Old Girls' Association and Interesting Ex-Pupils

The Association began in 1902 and the present Secretary is Josie Watts (Hewlett) who took over the post in March 1991. The previous Secretary was Jill Duffy (Knight 1954-61) and she recently described to me some of her thoughts about her 14 years in charge of the Association.

> *"I've met many Old Girls and corresponded with many others; what comes through clearly, time and time again, is an affection for the school and all that it has stood for throughout the years. Some memories are obviously very special…and most are connected with people: the school characters, especially staff who taught at K.H.S. for most of their working life, and whose influence has remained long after their pupils have left school. Listen to any conversation at an O.G.A. dinner and you will hear two things: first of all 'Do you remember Miss Doorly/Miss Springall/Miss Sunman/ Miss Garry/ Miss Whittlesey/ Miss Turley/Miss Browett etc. and then 'I must go and have a look at the Cottage/Eastgate/Landor and see if it's changed.'"*

King's High School has always enjoyed an excellent academic reputation and talented Old Girls are to be found in many varied walks of life.

Perhaps the best known ex-pupil is Barbara Ansell CBE (1930-1941) who has achieved international fame as a rheumatologist. After attending Birmingham Medical School and subsequently specialising in rheumatology, Barbara became a consultant in 1962. Barbara's own summary of her career leaves me in no doubt that it was her great energy and enthusiasm which helped to achieve success for her cause.

Barbara Ansell wrote to me in late 1993,

> *"From then on I continued, ending up as Head of the Division of Rheumatology at the Clinical Research Centre, Northwick Park Hospital, Harrow from 1975 to 1988. During that time we managed to establish paediatric rheumatology clinics*

*all over Great Britain and get interest from both the British Paediatric Association
and the British Society for Rheumatology. In addition I was the first chairman of
the working party and then of the full committee of the European League against
Rheumatism for work with paediatric rheumatology, and indeed only passed this
over relatively recently and have guided them to an international committee. I still
lecture widely in many parts of the world ... In addition I now have time to do a
lot of work for charities such as The Arthritis & Rheumatism Council, on whose
committees I sit and for Arthritis Care, the caring society for rheumatic diseases, the
Scleroderma Society and the Raynaud's and Scleroderma Association."*

Barbara was the daughter of Herbert Ansell, a past Mayor of Warwick who was
Secretary of Warwick Building Society for many years and also a Trustee of King
Henry Vlll's Charity. Her mother Annie (nee Chubb) was an Old Girl of K.H.S.
Although she has lived in Buckinghamshire for a number of years, Dr Ansell still
visits Warwick occasionally and is a member of the O.G.A.

Ironically whilst researching and writing this book, I suffered considerably from
osteo-arthritis and when consulting my own G.P. and a consultant rheumatologist
I mentioned my interest in Dr Ansell. Both doctors were most enthusiastic about
Dr Ansell's career and I was suitably impressed!

As one might expect teaching was a popular career choice, especially decades ago
and there have been numerous headteachers and heads of department amongst the
Old Girls. Pauline Molnar (Curson 1940-1947) was head of two schools, first
Langley Park School For Girls in Beckenham and later one of the early
Comprehensives Mayfield School in Putney.

Some in recent decades have become pioneers like Hilary Whiteway who in 1986
was a Squadron Leader in the R.A.F. and became the first woman to command an
operational unit in the Falklands, whilst others like Kim Hartman who played
Helga in 'Allo 'Allo! made acting or the performing arts their career.

Personally I am very interested in those who became writers and Maud Morin, who
attended the school in the 1880s and later became well known for writing school stories
such as "To the Fray St Agatha's" gave a speech and represented writers at the Jubilee
Celebrations of 1929. Mabel Ashby (1907-1911) well known for her work in
education, wrote several local history books and her biography of her father "Joseph
Ashby of Tysoe 1859 -1919" won the James Tait Black prize for the best biography of
1961. The late Frances O'Shaughnessey (Hill 1914-20) after retiring from her
headmistress's post in a local school, wrote local history books including "A Spa and Its
Children" which was published in 1979, besides assisting the Leamington Spa Literary
Society with other publications.

A contemporary of mine, Pauline Harris (1949-1956) after completing her
degree at Birmingham University and teaching for some years has written many
highly successful novels, under the pen names of Rachel Ford and Rebecca King,
which have been published in numerous countries. Harriet Castor (1986-1988) is
the author of several children's books including "Fat Puss and Friends" in 1984, and

"Fat Puss on Wheels" which was published whilst she was in the sixth form in 1987.

Some creative people such as Pamela Colebourn (1922-31) have become writers and artists. Pamela worked on various Fleet Street magazines and elsewhere both as a writer and an illustrator. She wrote a successful novel and now concentrates on painting, especially miniatures. Some of her designs have been featured by the large greetings card manufacturers and her current work, produced from her base in Eastbourne, is much in demand.

The Governors – Jean Constantine's Long Involvement

Since 1879 the King's High School has had a succession of conscientious Governors, many of whose daughters were educated in the school. Many Governors also served on the Board of Warwick School but although sometimes the girls' school felt second-best, there were always Governors who took a special interest in girls' education.

Sir Michael Lakin (a Governor from 1884 and Chairman from 1925-31) was very supportive as were Mr J.W. Mann (a Freeman of the Borough), Mr Lloyd Evans, Mrs Lloyd Evans, Mrs Pitman, and Mrs E.L. Tibbits who was Chairman at a difficult period in the 1940s. Mrs Ethel Brown M.B.E. was Chairman for a number of years until 1976, but in recent times nobody has had more involvement with the school in a variety of different capacities than long-standing Governor Dr Jean Constantine.

Having been a pupil from 1932 to 1946, much of the time under the influential headmistress Miss Doorly, after qualifying as a Doctor, Jean was later school medical officer from 1964 to 1988. When her daughter attended King's High School from 1968 to 1975, she saw life from a parent's angle and from 1966 to 1978 she was the Secretary of the Old Girls Association. From 1970 to the present time, she has been a Governor and from 1977 to 1990 she was Chairman. No wonder Dr Constantine says that the King's High School has been "*a second home to me throughout my life.*"

Of her role as Governor, Dr Constantine says that "*the position is a privilege and a pleasure, time consuming but rewarding. Governors must include men and women of wide ranging experience and expertise – in education, law, finance, industry and commerce, banking and public relations, as well as showing a good measure of common sense and knowledge of the school. Although thoughts must always be directed towards the future, constantly developing and adapting to frequently changing circumstances, it is helpful to have Governors (such as former pupils) who understand the ethos and background of the school.*"

Of financial considerations, Dr Constantine said "*It goes without saying that the financial assistance provided by King Henry VIII Charity, especially in recent years has proved invaluable in enabling King's High School to maintain its high standing in the local community and in the educational world beyond. Its continuation will undoubtedly be an important factor in its remaining there.*"

The Premises of the King's High School

There can be little doubt that the unusual, historic premises used by King's High School since its formation in 1879 has had a considerable effect on the pupils lucky enough to study there.

Landor House was built in 1692/3 when extensive alterations by carpenter Roger Hurlbutt (who completed much work at Warwick Castle together with his brother William) were made to a much older building on the site. Since I described the premises in detail in a previous book, local historian Steven Wallsgrove has drawn various interesting facts to my attention and I am very grateful to him and also to Dr Christine Hodgetts and Michael Farr, the ex-County archivist.

In 1482 the earlier property on the Landor House site was owned by Benedict Lee, a grazier who had been Master of the Warwick Guild in 1466. Some years later it became a large inn called the Maidenhead and around 1538, immediately prior to the dissolution of the monasteries, the Priory in Warwick owned the property which was held by Sir George Throckmorton. In 1544 he leased "The Maidenhead" and various other nearby properties, probably including the adjacent cottages, to John Ray and in 1604 Thomas Throckmorton sold the Maidenhead and other properties to Barnabie Holbarge and John Mawdick. The Maidenhead Inn seemed to be closely linked to St Mary's Church as visiting Bishops sometimes stayed there.

When I was writing the previous book, I felt convinced that Landor House and its predecessor had been used by those sympathetic to the Roman Catholic Church and the Jacobite cause. These recent findings could fit in with my theory and I remain convinced of the existence of a secret passage to St Mary's. A most interesting article in the Warwick Advertiser in 1946 described the legend of how such a tunnel ran under the Tinkertank … all I can comment is that stranger things have been found to be true.

The cottages adjacent to Landor House were first mentioned in 1482 when they were described as two tenements held by the Earl of Warwick and in a survey of 1575 they were owned by John Weale. In 1694 the cottages were purchased by Dr William Johnson, owner of Landor House and from 1733 both Landor House and the cottages were leased to support the charity for the poor begun by Ann Johnson, William's widow.

Both Landor House, where the poet Walter Savage Landor was born in 1775, and the adjoining cottages were given by the Trustees of Ann Johnson's Charity in 1877 to the Governors of the King's Schools and they have been used by King's High School since 1879.

Eastgate was first leased to the school in 1916 and although it is now in private hands the school still continues to rent the property.

Many of the letters I received about reminiscences of the school concerned the buildings and I thought readers would appreciate these three comments.

"You cannot imagine how much Landor House, the cottages and Eastgate meant to us as boarders, not being able to leave the building ... (Re Cottage Dormitory) The polished oak floors were so warped that the beds, having casters, moved considerably during the night as we turned over ... When the clock face on Eastgate was illuminated at night, we once saw the outline of a cat, so Mollie and I used to climb up the stairs where Mr Fallen went up to wind up the clock and took it food and milk ... It was a wonderful place to grow up as children. It was all so much part of our lives."

Joyce Kuhns (Jennings 1923-32)

"Our ghost, a lady in grey, walked through the old Cottage Dorm. and I swear passed the foot of my bed on more than one occasion. There were stories which abounded about a secret passage to St Mary's church and Fallen the caretaker showed us a bricked-in archway under the main staircase well.

Eastgate could be what my grand daughter calls 'spooky' on dark winter nights spent alone swotting for my 'Higher' in the top reference library, accompanied only by the ticking and striking of the clock and the moaning of the wind through the cracks in the windows and floorboards."

Glenys Phelps (Jones – Boarder 1925-1933)

Finally, a very special friend of mine, with whom I have corresponded regularly for nearly 40 years, Margaret Lang who taught English at K.H.S. from 1948 to 1960, described to me what it was like to live alone at weekends in the attics around 1950.

"The nights were quite eerie. There would be strange creaks on the polished floors of the upstairs landing as though someone was approaching and I would sit up in bed, full of apprehension. I used to leave on the light in the corridor but sometimes to my horror, the strip of light beneath the ill-fitting door would be blocked out. I imagine the sounds were made by the shrinkage of the wood as it cooled but I never discovered why the light disappeared."

WARWICK PREPARATORY SCHOOL

The school was created as an independent establishment as a result of the 1944 Education Act. Previous to that younger girls and a few boys had been catered for in the Kindergarten and Junior Department of the King's High School.

As a name the newly independent school took the title of the premises which it rented in The Butts, St Mary's Hall, and this name continued until a serious fire forced the school to move to new premises on the Banbury Road in 1971. Then known as Warwick Preparatory School, the Governors of the King's Schools bought back control on the retirement of Miss Smalley in 1966.

PUPILS OF ST MARY'S HALL PREPARATORY SCHOOL ENJOY SOME LIVELY GAMES IN THE SUMMER OF 1955. The building to the right had once been Warwick Technical School and that to the left, part of the King's Middle School. The Preparatory School rented rooms from St Mary's Church which had purchased the premises in 1910. Mrs Pritchard, the present headmistress of Warwick Preparatory School, commented "These children could be in our playground now. The same dateless dresses with white collars and cuffs and gathered skirts still form part of our uniform." (King's High School Archives)

Early Beginnings Pre 1944

As with many Secondary Schools set up in the later nineteenth century, the King's High School For Girls soon felt the need to cater for younger pupils. So in 1887 a Kindergarten Department was established as a department of the main school.

In the early years the younger pupils used the large upper room in Landor House, which is now a staff room. Girls and a few boys were admitted from around the age of five and they were taught in small classes until they were old enough to join the main school. At the age of seven, the boys mostly transferred to the Junior Department of Warwick School.

In 1916, when space was short as the numbers of pupils had increased overall, Eastgate was leased and the Kindergarten Department moved in there, using the outside stone steps as a separate access. Recently I have spoken with two ex-kindergarten pupils concerning this period and Mary and Margaret Stiles (now Mrs Woodall and Mrs Thomas) vividly recalled having lessons in 1917 in the Coaching Room above the pedestrian arch in Eastgate.

In 1918 when the Technical School building to the rear of the old Middle School became vacant, the Juniors were able to move in and there they stayed for the next 50 years and more. In 1906 the old Middle School had been closed and in 1911 the entire site, including the Technical School which continued to function till 1918, had been sold to St Mary's Church which needed parish rooms for Sunday Schools and other meetings. However almost from the start, the premises proved too large for exclusive church use and rooms were rented first to the Senior Department of King's High School and later to the Junior Department.

Miss Smalley First Headmistress

Gweneth Kathleen Smalley, who came from Peterborough, was first appointed to teach the Kindergarten Department of the King's High School in September 1934. She continued running this department until headmistress Miss Doorly retired at Chirstmas 1944 and the implications of the 1944 Education Act meant that the Junior Department, along with the boarding house, would have to be closed.

In order to save the school, Miss Smalley bought it herself and ran it as an independent Preparatory School. Two of the King's High School staff, Miss Davidson a music teacher and Miss Edwards who was able to teach needlework, joined Miss Smalley and they were soon joined by three other staff including Miss Allibon, an Old Girl of King's High School (1931-39).

During its first independent year, the school had to develop its own uniform, administration and badge. For this Miss Smalley, who like Miss Davidson was a keen naturalist, made the inspired choice of a red squirrel with an acorn which was a symbol of knowledge. (Mighty oaks from little acorns etc.)

By all accounts Miss Smalley was very talented in many respects, but she was essentially a private person, even with her closest colleagues. In her younger days Miss Smalley had been a mountain climber and all her life she was a keen bird watcher. Particularly friendly with Miss Davidson who shared many of her interests, the two of them would often embark on nature excursions together.

Miss Smalley continued as headmistress until 1966 when she retired. Miss Davidson retired early through ill health in 1971 and she eventually died in 1981 aged 69.

Following retirement, Miss Smalley was elected to Leamington Town Council soon afterwards and she remained a member for many years, eventually becoming an Alderman. Her retirement was an active one and she indulged in numerous hobbies such as woodwork.

In 1989 she opened the new nursey block at the school, then securely established in its new premises near Warwick School, and this must have been a very proud day for her. When she died in 1991 at the age of 88, she left a legacy of £5,000 to the "Squirrels" – having done more than anyone else to ensure the future of the school which had formed so great a part of her life.

THIS DELIGHTFUL SNAP SHOWING MISS DAVIDSON (LEFT) MISS SMALLEY (CENTRE) AND MISS ALLIBON WAS TAKEN IN THE 1950s. The three were obviously enjoying their hand-bell practice, but unfortunately the photographer forgot the basic rule about obscuring a person's face! I am assured that the same hand-bells are still in frequent use today at Warwick Preparatory School. (NA)

Miss Allibon and Transition Years

Nancy Allibon was connected with the Preparatory School nearly all her life and she taught there for 36 years; for 14 of those years she was deputy headmistress.

She had assisted with the Kindergarten Department whilst she was still in the sixth form at King's High School. After going to college and beginning her career at Bath Place School in Leamington, she was invited to join the newly independent Preparatory School at Christmas 1945. For the next 36 years Miss Allibon gave invaluable service to the school, seeing it through some of its most traumatic times when space was short which necessitated her teaching some of the younger pupils in Bridge House, near Warwick School from 1967.

In November 1970 the horrific fire in St Mary's Hall meant that a vast amount of equipment and records were lost, and also rendered the older pupils without premises. The Warwick Schools Foundation had bought the Bridge House site some years earlier and provided the Preparatory School with a site at Bridge Field on which new buildings could be erected. Already planned when the fire occurred the building programme was embarked on quickly.

In 1971 some of the new premises including 4 new classrooms were opened by Viscount Radcliffe and Miss Allibon helped supervise the move, her experience proving invaluable to headmistress Mrs Hogan and newer members of staff.

When Miss Allibon retired in 1981 amongst her retirement presents was a most unusual piece of pottery, made by pupils, which showed children with guinea pigs and squirrels. The significance of the squirrels were obvious but the guinea pigs were there because she had always looked after those at school and the children often believed that she could speak to them!

I was most impressed when I visited Miss Allibon recently when she showed me several treasured items which had once belonged to Miss Smalley. A wonderful corner cupboard, carefully made from tulip wood had pride of place and there was also an elegant mirror in bands of contrasting wood. Amazingly both items had been made by Miss Smalley during her retirement. Ex-pupils would have been glad to see that a Kate Greenway Birthday Book inscribed "*To G.K. Smalley with love and best wishes from her school Christmas 1945*" was still treasured.

As she described Miss Smalley and her other ex-colleagues, Miss Allibon made me feel the enormous pride and love the staff at that time had felt for their school and I thought what a wonderful beginning this set of talented teachers had given Warwick Preparatory School.

CIVIC RESPONSIBILITIES

Although there was no Civic expenditure specified in the original Letters Patent which set up the Charity, when the Guild of Warwick passed over its properties in June 1545, the Corporation was then bound to carry out the Civic obligations previously administered by the Guild. Such obligations included the maintenance of the Great Bridge, Eastgate, Westgate, the Guildhall (later the Court House) and the repair of certain roads.

In the early years of the Corporation there were attempts to keep the various accounts separate and the Charity of King Henry VIII(for church and school) was kept separate from the Guild Account (for Civic affairs). Likewise the Bailiff's Account (the market tolls) created by the Charter of 1554 for Civic entertaining was supposed to be kept separate. However as time went on all assets and obligations were lumped together under the general title of the Charity of King Henry VIII. So this Estate funded all Corporation liabilities, helped by a little money from a few other sources such as private legacies and Charities such as Oken's which deliberately overlapped with Civic business and which were administered by Aldermen of the Corporation.

Although in 1637 the Bailiff had been granted a stipend of £20 per annum to help with entertaining and other Civic expenses, from 1777 stipends had also been granted to other Corporation officials. From 1777 the Mayor's stipend was increased from £30 to £100 and the Town Clerk was granted £15, the Sergeant at Mace £15, the Yeoman £10 and the Beadle £5. These stipends were not the only source of income for these officials, they merely augmented other privileges and sources of income which these Corporation officials possessed.

By a Decree dated 1818 the Corporation stipends were increased ... the Mayor being granted £150 instead of £100, the Town Clerk £25 instead of £15, the Sergeant at Mace £20 instead of £15, the Yeoman £15 instead of £10 and the Beadle £10 instead of £5. It would appear that the Beadle fulfilled some of the duties of a caretaker and part of his responsibilities were to keep the Court House clean and wait on the Mayor and Corporation.

The Great Bridge Over the Avon

One of the most important areas of maintenance for which the Corporation was liable was that of the Great Bridge over the River Avon near Warwick Castle, for this bridge was vital to the town.

From early times, the Guild of Warwick had been responsible for the repair of the 100 yards long, stone bridge with 12 or 13 arches which spanned the Avon near

THIS TRANQUIL GARDEN IN MILL STREET WITH THE ADJACENT RUINS OF THE MEDIEVAL BRIDGE IS ONE OF MY FAVOURITE PLACES IN WARWICK. The Mill Garden is frequently open to the public and as a result the generous owner has raised thousands of pounds for local charities. (JF)

the Castle at the bottom of Mill Street. The stone bridge, erected around 1375 or before, replaced an earlier one in all likelihood built of wood which was in use by 1200. Previous to that bridge it seems probable that the river, which was wider and shallower than today was forded near the castle. From 1375 the inhabitants of Warwick were allowed to collect a tax from users to pay for repairs of the bridge and the responsibility for the upkeep eventually fell to the United Guild of Warwick. So when the Guild of Warwick handed over its assets, the upkeep of the great bridge was included in the responsibilities given to the Corporation of the town.

Those who wish to see for themselves exactly what the bridge was like have only to visit its remains, now adjacent to the fine garden belonging to Mr Arthur Measures at 55 Mill Street. I never tire of visiting this beautiful garden which is frequently open to the public with the proceeds going to various charities.

To sit in the peace of Arthur Measures' garden and gaze at the ruins of the old bridge, is to capture the spirit of past centuries in one's imagination. Pack-horses laden with cloth, fine carriages carrying wealthy travellers, poorer townfolk scurrying about their daily business – all crossed the narrow bridge close to the castle.

Some idea of the exact site of the old bridge can be obtained from reference to a map compiled by James Fish in 1711. The bridge was situated almost at the bottom of Mill Street and there was direct access from St Mary's and the centre of Warwick via Castle Street, the remains of which can be seen near Oken's House. The end of the old bridge was fairly close to Guy's Tower so that the huge might of the Castle dominated the view of those crossing into Warwick. On the south side, the village of Bridge End was exactly what its name suggests. The Southam Road (Myton Road), Itchington Road (Harbury Lane) and the Banbury Road all converged in Bridge End, near to the bridge so that village must have possessed great strategic value.

WARWICK CASTLE AND THE GREAT BRIDGE AS PAINTED (BY JAMES FISH?) IN THE EARLY 18TH CENTURY. The painting from which this photograph is taken hangs in the Shire Hall, but there is another similar oil painting in Fulke Greville's Study in the Watergate Tower of Warwick Castle. The surveyor James Fish completed a signed engraving which is again similar in age and composition. (Reproduced by permission of Warwickshire County Record Office)

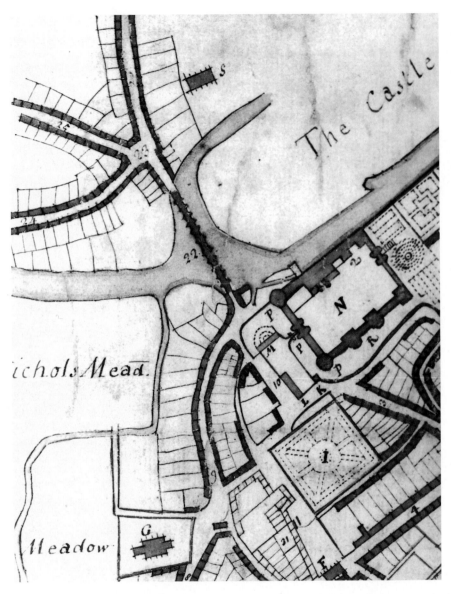

THIS MAP OF 1711 BY JAMES FISH CLEARLY SHOWS THE POSITION OF THE GREAT BRIDGE.........MARKED 22 ON THE MAP. The Castle courtyard is labelled N, the Castle towers P, the vineyard garden I, St Nicholas Church G, Eastgate F, Castle Street 3 and Mill Street 9. To the south (unusually at the top) 23 marks the position of the village of Bridge End S is the Temple Chapel. (Reproduced by permission of Warwickshire County Record Office)

*THIS FAMOUS WATERCOLOUR WARWICK CASTLE AND BRIDGE PAINTED BY J.M.W.
TURNER IN 1794 IS THOUGHT BY MANY TO REFLECT THE INFLUENCE OF
CANALETTO ON THE YOUNG ENGLISH ARTIST. (By courtesy of the Whitworth Art Gallery,
University of Manchester)*

New Bridge Proposed

By the mid 18th century, the old bridge, like so many other similar structures in
other towns, was needing frequent repair, and various proposals were put forward
for the building of a new one.

In his "History of the Charity of Henry VIII" E.G. Tibbits said that from
medieval times the bridge had been a *"great financial burden to the town."* The
scouring effect of the river water and occasional floods meant that costly repairs were
often necessary.

By the 1770s the Corporation, as Trustees of King Henry VIII Charity, seemed
agreed that a new bridge was needed and various schemes were put forward.
However it must be borne in mind that the Corporation had only recently had the
income from Henry VIII's Estate returned to its control after the sequestration of
1737. Although there were now few debts, there was little money to pay for a brand
new bridge.

UNTIL RECENT TIMES THE LIVES OF THE INHABITANTS OF WARWICK WERE DOMINATED BY THE CASTLE AND ITS RULERS. This engraving of 1814 illustrates how everyone who approached the town from the south would have been subtly reminded of the might of the Castle every time they crossed the Great Bridge. After the Great Bridge was replaced in 1793, the remains became this picturesque ruin. (Reproduced by permission of Warwickshire County Record Office)

The Second Earl of Warwick, George Greville (1773-1816) had great plans for enlarging the grounds of his Castle and a scheme was drawn up proposing that a new bridge be built downstream. The main roads into Warwick from the south could then be rebuilt, so that far more town land could be enclosed within the Castle walls.

Eventually an Act of Parliament dated 1788 empowered George to build a bridge within 3 years, he then paying for the maintenance for the next 7 years (a negligible amount if the bridge was built properly?). Then the Corporation would resume control and responsibility and pay for repairs from King Henry VIII's Charity once again.

The New Castle Bridge

In 1776 Leafield Bridge, which is situated within the Castle Estate, was completed and although there is no firm documentary evidence, it seems likely that it was a prototype for the new public bridge over the Avon. In recent times, part of the Leafield Bridge has fallen away and it has become clear that there are a series of vaults lying from side to side under the road in the fabric of the bridge. An unusual design, it is slightly smaller than Castle Bridge which has a greater width.

THE FIGURES IN THE FOREGROUND MAKE THIS ENGRAVING OF WARWICK CASTLE AND THE NEW CASTLE BRIDGE FAR MORE INTERESTING. Depicting life in the early 19th century, this is one of my favourite illustrations of old Warwick. (Reproduced by permission of Warwickshire County Record Office)

THIS DRAWING FROM THE AYLESFORD COLLECTION SHOWS WESTGATE AND THE LORD LEYCESTER HOSPITAL IN 1821. Around 1830 the roads and pavements near Westgate were widened and vastly improved, the expenses being met largely from the Charity of King Henry VIII. (Reproduced by permission of Birmingham City Archives)

The new Castle Bridge was begun in 1789. The stone was carried down the river in boats from the Rock Mill Quarry at Emscote and for around 4 years, the area from Eastgate, down Castle Hill as far as the Banbury Road on the far side of Bridge End was a huge building site. For the inhabitants of the time, it must have been a terrible upheaval.

Thomas Kemp in his "History of Warwick and Its People" quotes the following dates which he says were from an old book in St Nicholas' vestry. *August 1st 1789 The first stone of the Butment of the new bridge was laid by Eboral the Mason. May 26 1791 The last stone was laid of the arch of the new bridge in St Nicholas Meadow.*

To put affairs in Warwick into their historical place ... the new bridge was begun just 16 days after the start of the French Revolution when the Bastille was stormed on 14th July 1789. However communications being relatively poor in those times, I expect few in Warwick bothered about affairs on the continent when William Eboral laid the first stone.

The bridge is an elegant one and the span of the arch measures 105 feet. Almost certainly the temporary timber supports used for the construction of Leafield Bridge were re-used in the construction of Castle Bridge although the latter is bigger, being 36 feet wide, 25 feet high. It is said that each stone weighed from 2,000 to 3,000 pounds.

A graceful structure, the new bridge immediately began to inspire artists and masters such as William Mallord Turner painted the dramatic scene from St Nicholas Meadow where the new bridge outlined the castle. The fact that the central arches of the old bridge were soon washed away by floods helped to dramatise the scene and many contemporary magazines had engravings of the Avon at Warwick. The view of the Castle and ruins of the old bridge were ideally seen from the centre of the new bridge and soon travellers such as Sir Walter Scott were saying that the scene was the finest view in England.

As to cost, the new bridge cost around £4,000 and of this the Earl of Warwick paid £3,000. The remaining £1,000 was to be found from King Henry VIII's Charity, but by 1800 this money had not been paid.

In his "History of the Charity of King Henry VIII" E.G. Tibbits described the end of this particular story. By 1923 the stone balusters were very worn and the Charity Trustees asked the County bridgemaster to advise. In 1929 £750 was spent on repairs but in 1931 the Trustees enquired whether the County Council would accept responsibility for the bridge, as it already maintained the road which crossed it. The Charity Commissioners were approached and eventually all parties agreed that as the bridge had originally been the responsibility of the inhabitants at large, it was correct that the County Council should assume responsibility. So on 9th May 1934 the Trustees eventually relinquished control of what E.G. Tibbits had called "*a headache for centuries*".

Some of the facts about Castle Bridge seem almost stranger than fiction. In 1940 when a German invasion was feared, it was secretly made ready to be blown up, as it was in a most important position. It was said that dynamite was placed in secret places in the bridge, but until recently this was doubted. Now it has been realised that Castle Bridge was constructed in a similar way to Lea Field Bridge, probably with a similar system of interior vaults, more credence has been given to the story. Also there is evidence in the County Council's Drawing Record that a large part of the West parapet was taken down during the Second World War as part of defensive works. It was rumoured that the parapet was replaced with sand bags, effectively fortifying the bridge.

In recent years the bridge has been surveyed and calculations made to determine its carrying capacity. It says much for the abilities of the designer (Robert Mylne?) and the builders for it has been found to be perfectly adequate to accept modern day traffic of a weight and volume inconceivable in 1789 when construction commenced.

For much of this section concerning bridges, I am indebted to Michael Sharman, Chief Bridge Consultant for Warwickshire County Council and his enthusiasm inspired me to seek out fresh information.

Roads and Pavements

Not only was the Corporation liable for keeping the bridges in repair, but certain roads and paved areas also had to be maintained.

The earliest account book which I read contained many bills and receipts dated around 1622, bound into one volume. There were several repairs to the Great Bridge with various charges for stones and lime, but there were also bills for pebbles for paving.

Over the centuries, there were many repairs needed for Wedgnock Lane towards Hatton, so much so that a special field on the northern outskirts of Warwick was set aside for grazing the oxen which drew the carts carrying the stones and other materials. Other roads in the town, too, often had grants towards their maintenance.

In 1805 some roads around the Market Place and Saltisford were widened and between 1808 and 1811 the roads round Eastgate were improved and culverted, those around Westgate being widened and paved from 1816-18. Gradually the narrow and picturesque streets disappeared and the town's roads took on the appearance they have today.

John Loudon Macadam (1756-1836) was a Scot who did much to improve the condition of English roads in the first third of the 19th century. He invented a method of making roads smoother by first improving drainage and then applying a mixture which solidified the road with a mixture of tar and hard, small stones. Between 1828-1830 the roads on either side of West Gate (West Street and High Street) ... the steep hill on the approach to Warwick from the West were macadamised. The roads in question were ultimately the responsibility of the surveyors of the highways of St Mary's parish, but in 1830 the Corporation made a grant of £30 towards Macadamizing the hill at St James' Chapel near Westgate.

We assume that compulsory orders for road widening to be a modern idea, but they certainly happened in past centuries One entry in the Accounts Book for 1816-1817 was *"To Mr Eyres for the purchase of and taking down part of a house at the top of West Street near the West Street Chapel for the purpose of widening the road there – £205 4sh 0d.*

Street Lighting.

It was definitely bad news for sperm whales and seals when Warwick Corporation decided to use some of the profits from King Henry VIIIs Estate to pay for oil lamps to light the streets in 1803.

The idea had been mooted for several months, but in 1803 a formal objection by an influential group of Warwick residents, largely Whig supporters, sought to prevent the Corporation from *"applying part of the income arising from King Henry VIII's Estates for the purpose of lighting the Public Streets of the town."* The concept of organised lighting in many streets was a new idea and as it cost several hundred pounds, the objectors doubtless felt that with so many poor and starving people in the town, the money could have been better spent.

However the Mayor, William Birch, called a meeting to discuss the objection and in January 1803 the Corporation restated their intention to proceed with the proposals. The Account Books of 1804 and 1805 carry several details of the new street lighting. Lamp irons were supplied and painted and John Walker paid for lamp oil and for lighting the streets. In 1805 John Walker was paid £211 3sh 0d for lamp oil, wickyarn and lighting the streets, but it seems that his efforts were not entirely satisfactory.

In 1806 a Contract Is Signed With a London Firm

A fascinating document dated 7th August 1806 gave details of an agreement between William Couldery & Son of Whitecross Street, Cripplegate, London and the Corporation. A public notice had been placed in Aris's Birmingham Gazette and in Warwick inviting *"proposals to be delivered in by any Person or Persons willing to contract for the cleaning and lighting of the lamps of the town."* I found the idea that the street lighting project had to be in effect "put out to tender" in itself amusing as it is always assumed to be a modern concept, but I suppose the answer was that local firms had insufficient expertise to accept a contract. In 1806 the use of oil lamps for street lighting was a modern idea, only made possible by improved technology from 1780 onwards concerning glass covered lamps and the development of the use of whale and seal oil.

I do not know how many replies the Corporation had to the notices, but in 1806 they signed the agreement with William Couldery and Thomas Sims Couldery of White Cross Street, Cripplegate, London   to supply and maintain street oil lamps for a period of 7 years. Either a "one spout two lens burner (Patent) or a two spout one double convex lens burner" was to be supplied at various locations and spermaceti and seal oil mixed in equal quantities was to be burned.

The idea that improved shipping practices in the late eighteenth century meant that whales and seals were being killed in large quantities to provide English towns with street lights was extremely repugnant and it was something which had never before ocurred to me. Nineteenth century reference books describe how spermaceti was obtained from the heads of sperm whales and I must say I felt ashamed to think that my own area was partly responsible for the catastrophic decline in numbers of these wonderful mammals. Begun around 1775, the sperm whale trade in the Pacific and Indian Oceans alone engaged 75 English ships by 1791, nearly all of them based in the London docks. In 1806 Whitecross Street was handily placed for the import of whale and seal oil, being perhaps 4 miles away from the London docks.

The terms of the contract I found most amusing. The lamps were to be lit every night for 6 months of the year until 2 a.m. except for 7 nights every full moon. Quite what happened on overcast nights was not specified! For each lamp put up and taken down in the spring, the Corporation paid 16sh 6d (82^1/2p) but the contractors were to be deducted 2d per night per lamp for every lamp not lighted. To avoid draughts and to provide better illumination, the ultra modern lamps had glass covers and special wicks. For each glass which was broken, the Corporation had to pay 9sh 6d … so street fights and loutish behaviour had to be prevented.

Whitecross Street, Cripplegate

In many ways it is the seemingly trivial documents such as these which bring history to life – even the address of the Couldery Partners proved most interesting.

Cripplegate, one of the ancient gates of the City of London, gave its name to the area and Whitecross Street, named after an ancient priory, extended from Fore Street near London Wall as far as Old Street. In Shakespearian times (around 1600) the Fortune Theatre was built in Whitecross Street by Edward Alleyne and today a plaque on the corner of Whitecross and Fortune Street commemorates this. The ancient church of St Giles without Cripplegate, where Sir Thomas More worshipped, Oliver Cromwell was married and John Milton was buried, still lies close to London Wall and in 1806 the yard occupied by the Couldery family would have been close to the church.

Contact with the Guildhall Librarian and Borough Librarian of Islington Council (Finsbury) has confirmed that the Couldery family occupied premises in Greenyard, Whitecross Street … the area where stray cattle from the city were pounded and the Lord Mayor's state coach was kept.

Today only part of Whitecross Street remains … the area where Greenyard was situated is now part of the massive but extremely interesting Barbican Development. However further along Whitecross Street there remains a Dickensian-looking cul-de-sac named Warwick Yard which dates from 1814, which I like to think may have some connection with the Couldery family who doubtless made large profits from their contract with Warwick Corporation.

However some inhabitants felt that the 30 shillings weekly which was spent on street lights in the first two decades of the nineteenth century could have made a huge difference to the thousands of starving people in Warwick at that time. On page 76 of his "History of Warwick and its People" Thomas Kemp, probably without realising it, explained the street lamps controversy. On one hand he spoke of Hunt Balls for the rich folk in the Court House, with the ladies being conducted in the small hours of the morning to the Warwick Arms for supper hence the need for street lights? On the other hand during the winter of 1816/7, 4,000 starving people in Warwick were each served twice a week with soup and a slice of bread.

The contract for oil lamps in the streets was renewed in 1812 for a further period and in 1815-1816 for example William Couldery and his son were paid £213 3sh 6d for lighting the town.

It was not until March 1822 that the town was partially lighted with gas and still the Corporation continued to pay for the street lighting from the profits from the Estate of King Henry VIII. From 1st September 1829 to 2nd April 1830 the Corporation paid Warwick Gas Company £357 19sh 5d for lighting the streets.

Policing

From Elizabethan times, each parish was required to have a constable who carried out various duties. However in the early 19th century, matters were so serious in

Warwick that the Corporation was asked to help. £100 was paid to J. Hickling in 1819 "*acting on behalf of the inhabitants of the Borough for preventing a continuance of the nightly depredations committed on their property within the Borough.*" Elsewhere in England in 1819, there was similar political agitation and near Manchester in that year the infamous "Peterloo Massacre" when mounted yeomanry killed 9 and injured 600 of the crowd which had assembled to listen to political speeches, took place. In Warwick the money paid in 1819 went to provide night watchmen and such expenditure continued until 1827/8 when £200 was allotted. The extra £100 was paid to Thomas Bellerby as being the superintendent of the Watch.

Bread for the Poor

From 1545 to 1835 some of the criticisms of the way the Corporation ran the town's affairs centred on the choice of items funded and the lack of money which was given to the poor.

As lay rector of St Mary's and St Nicholas the Corporation did have an obligation to help the poor and this was also stipulated in the Decree of 1618. They were supposed to give at least £16 per year to the poor and to raise £100 to bind out apprentices. However they did little if anything and the Decree of 1638 concerning the Charity of King Henry VIII reaffirmed the commitment.

Still very little was done, but in the period when the Corporation lost control of the Charity, from 1742 to 1769, £52 a year was given towards poor relief, with extra if necessary.

In the Account Books, for example that of 1753, the actual names of 54 poor or aged persons who had been given bread were listed. Bread to the total value of £1 was distributed every Sunday following morning service at St Mary's and St Nicholas

The times in the latter years of the 18th century and the first half of the 19th century were very difficult indeed for many of the population. A rapid increase in population and improvements in agriculture and mechanisation meant that the wages of many workers fell, whilst the price of corn and bread was kept high by the outdated Corn Laws. Many families were starving often through no fault of their own and many tenants could not afford to pay their rents. In some years, 1795 and 1816/7 particularly, there were huge numbers of starving people in the town. A subscription fund was set up in 1816/7 and to this the Corporation contributed £105 2sh 6d.

However when you consider that this sum was less than half that spent on lighting the streets with oil lamps, it would appear that the original objectors to the street lighting had a point. Had the Corporation got its priorities wrong? There were many who thought that the profits of King Henry VIII Charity was not being spent with regard to the well being of the majority of the inhabitants of Warwick.

THIS PICTURE EXPLAINS WHY KING HENRY VIII'S CHARITY HAD TO PAY THE SUM OF £6 13sh 8d ANNUALLY TO THE PENDRELL FAMILY AND THEIR DESCENDENTS FOR OVER 300 YEARS. King Charles II was helped to change his clothes at Whiteladies Priory near Wolverhampton and escape capture after his defeat at the Battle of Worcester in 1651, by Richard Pendrell and his family. After the Restoration, King Charles II rewarded the Pendrell family with a pension, part of which came from a fee farm rent payable to the Crown from King Henry VIII's Charity. (By courtesy of the National Portrait Gallery, London)

Other Payments.

Perhaps it would be more interesting to readers if I list a few actual payments to illustrate the diversity of the Civic causes which benefited from money from King Henry VIII's Charity.

1622 *"Bottle of Clarrit and pound of sugar for the Judges – 4sh 3d." (This was only one of many such payments for hospitality for the Judges of the Assizes over the centuries.)*

1753 *"To Thomas Wright for repairing the publick pavement in the Mens Market, Barley Market, Women's Market and Rear of church ... £25 10sh 7d."*

1794 *"To Jacob Grant a bill for weeding the pavement near St Mary's Church 4sh 8d"*

1794 *"To the expenses of several gentlemen of the Corporation going to view the estates at Chaddesley Corbett ... £17 6sh 0d"*

1815 *"To John Mills a bill for gravel used and for spreading the same on the new bridge ... £11 1sh 4d."*

1816 *"To Henry Sharpe a bill for printing and advertising ... £10 17sh."*

1829 *"To Edward Dodd a bill for coals used at the Court House by the Corporation at Sessions ... £4 2sh 9d."*

1829 *"To Messrs Jones, Palmer & Co, a bill for a carpet to the room for the Magistrates of the Borough ... £2 7sh 6d."*

The Accounts Books show various payments in connection with fire precautions. In 1829 Edward Taylor was paid £187 3sh 2d for making a fire engine and repairing the old engines and in 1817 £24 18sh 2d was paid to the Mayor's Fund for the expense of providing 50 fire buckets. Also in 1817 John Williams was paid £8 11sh for fire ladders for each ward of the town.

As directed by the Decree of 1637, the entries for each year in the Account Books were scrutinized and signed by two Justices of the Peace, one chosen by the Mayor and Corporation and the other chosen by the vicar of St Mary's. I was most interested to see that the entries for several years in the 1790s had been signed by Dr Walter Landor, J.P. father of the poet Walter Savage Landor. For many years wealthy Dr Landor and his family had rented Landor House from Ann Johnson's Charity and for decades he had practiced medicine in Warwick.

1836 and afterwards

Once the running of King Henry VIII's Charity had been placed in the hands of Trustees separate from the elected Council, the whole concept of Civic expenditure began to change. Various Committees were set up within the Council to administer the various departments – a Finance Committee being set up in 1836 ... From 1837 the balance of the surplus income from the Charity was transferred to the Borough Fund which then allotted money to the different departments.

In 1838 the first Borough Rate of $1^1/2$d in the £ was levied and gradually these Borough Rates became more and more important. During the 1830s and 1840s there was often friction between the Council and the Trustees of King Henry VIII's Charity and following a row in 1840 the Trustees refused to pay for the Watch Committee which ran the Police force. Eventually the Council used other Charity money and for a time Oken's Charity made payments instead.

Throughout much of the 19th century, King Henry VIII's Charity still handed over to the Borough Fund whatever was left after necessary expenditure on the churches and Grammar School, but the onus of responsibility regarding certain Civic funds was removed from the Trustees. This period from 1840 onwards was the time when education was to the forefront and the Trustees had many decisions to make concerning the King's School and its funding. Once the King's Schools Foundation had taken money and land from the main fund, King Henry VIII's Charity gradually declined in importance as profits decreased in the twentieth century. Much property had been sold in the period between 1877 and 1901, with the proceeds being invested in Consols (Government stock) but of the properties which remained many were old and needed costly repairs. So the importance of the Charity was diminished and for much of the 20th century, the distributable income was not even sufficient to pay the stipends to the clergy or pay much into the town.

THE MOST UNUSUAL PAYMENT OF ALL? THE PENDRELL GRANT.

In 1983 soon after he took over as Clerk of the Charity, Mr P.G. Butler was somewhat surprised to receive a letter from a solicitor in Wolverhampton asking for a small payment.

Mr K.S.P. Swayne of the firm of Fowler, Langley and Wright in Wolverhampton wrote,

"I am the receiver in respect of the Pendrell Grant which was made by King Charles II in 1676 to reward the Pendrell family who aided his escape after the battle of Worcester in 1651. I enclose a photographic extract from the copy of the Pendrell Grant which I hold and which was made in 1754 and this shows the creation of the Fee Farm Rent and exactly what it was charged upon ... You will appreciate that these Fee Farm Rents have been paid continuously since 1676 and in fact for the last 25 years I have been collecting this one from Mr Blenkinsop!"

It is quite true that the truth is often stranger than fiction and so it seems with the reason for the payment of the Pendrell Grant.

The Escape of King Charles II

In the evening of 3rd September 1651, having finally acknowledged defeat in the bloody battle of Worcester, the latter stages of which had been fought in the streets, the 21 year old King Charles II slipped quietly out of the north gate of the city, attended only by a few trustworthy lords.

In the darkness, uncertain of where to go, Catholic Charles Giffard eventually suggested isolated Whiteladies House, near to his own estate of Boscobel in Shropshire. Boscobel House, like Whiteladies, was let to members of the Pendrell (often spelt Penderel) family who were Catholic yeoman farmers. During the entire time that King Charles was in the area, the Pendrell family, including 5 brothers, their aged mother, their sister and her husband did all they could to help.

At Whiteladies, the tallest brother William Pendrell, gave country clothes to the 6 feet 2 inches tall king, helping him to be disguised as a woodman. After leaving Whiteladies John Pendrell acted as scout whilst Richard Pendrell alone accompanied the king. Unable to break out of the area, for all river crossings were watched, the pair had to ford a river to double back to Boscobel, which originally had been a hunting lodge in the middle of a thick forest. Arriving very early in the morning, King Charles did not dare remain in the house so he joined a Major Careless in a large and bushy pollard oak about 500 yards from the house. This oak afterwards became famous, with the king sleeping for much of the day, with his head on a cushion provided by the Pendrells, whilst Cromwell's soldiers roamed about searching the woods below.

The king spent the night in Boscobel House his long body squeezed into a priests' hiding hole (which is still in existence) after Humphrey Pendrell had described how there was a huge price of £1,000 on the king's head. The following day, Richard and George Pendrell and the other brothers, together with Francis Yates their brother-in-law, conveyed the king to Moseley Old Hall near Wolverhampton (now National Trust Property) where he had to use another secret hiding place when soldiers searched the premises. King Charles eventually escaped the net of troops thanks largely to a brave woman named Jane Lane, who disguised him as her servant. After numerous adventures, the king arrived in France, but all the Pendrells repeatedly had their houses searched and their remaining possessions confiscated. Francis Yates, the husband of Elizabeth Pendrell, was hanged at Oxford soon afterwards for his part in the escape.

In happier times, after the Restoration in 1660, King Charles rewarded the 60 or so people to whom he owed his life. Some were granted a pension and amongst these were the 5 Pendrell brothers and their married sister Elizabeth Yates. The famous Boscobel oak (a sapling of which still remains to this day near to the house which is open to the public) really captured the public's imagination and the Royal Tree was commemorated each year on King Charles II's birthday 29th May, which became a public holiday known as Oak Apple Day. The day was observed for around 200 years and only fell into obscurity in the mid nineteenth century.

The Fee Farm Rent 1676 to 1988.

Although he received the Pendrells at Court and helped their children, King Charles II ensured the pensions (at no cost to the Exchequer or himself) by the creation of a large number of fee farm rents, the money from which was to be paid via Trustees to the Pendrell family and their decendents in perpetuity. The fee farm rent – Number 50 – said to issue out of the rectory of St Nicholas and St Mary in Warwick was payable by the Burgesses of Warwick.

The annual amount was £6 13sh 4d and this was paid by King Henry VIII's Charity for the next 312 years towards the Pendrell pensions or annuities. However, following an order of Chancery in 1921, which enabled these fee farm rents to be redeemed this particular rent was redeemed in 1988 and King Henry VIII's Charity had to purchase consolidated stock in the name of the Pendrell Trustees to produce the same income as previously. So for the sum of £170.35 in 1988, a release was obtained and this wonderful tale of bravery and just reward ceased to have any connection with Warwick.

I am indebted to Mr K.P.S. Swayne (now retired) for describing many of the legal aspects of this story which seemed to me to embody all that was best concerning English History and the English legal system, even if the Corporation and inhabitants of Warwick were called upon to help reward favours given to a king.

Various Letters Connecting the London Church of St Giles in the Fields with Warwick

Much of the information I have given here concerning the escape of King Charles II originated from biographies of the king, in particular those written by Antonia Fraser aand Arthur Bryant. However amongst the vast number of documents connected with King Henry VIII's Charity in Warwickshire County Record Office is a fascinating bundle of letters connected with the Pendrell Trust.

In October 1930 Warwick solicitors Heath and Blenkinsop, the Receivers and Treasurers for King Henry VIII Charity, enquired from Inge & Son of Lichfield as to the exact reason for the small annual payment made to the Pendrell Trustees. The reply came from Charles W. Giffard Inge, whom I believe was a descendent of the Charles Giffard who had owned Boscobel House in the seventeenth century.

In 1946 W. Kent (the editor of "Encyclopaedia of London") wrote to "The Times" newspaper asking if any pensions were still paid to the descendents of Richard Pendrell whose tomb could still be seen in the churchyard of St Giles in the Fields in London.

Naturally Heath and Blenkinsop replied saying that Warwick Borough (through King Henry VIII's Charity) still paid a half yearly sum to the Pendrell Trust.

Eventually, later in 1946, there was a second letter in "The Times" from W. Kent and he stated that he had been informed that in 1675 Charles II granted 6 pensions to the widow and heirs of Richard Pendrell. There were a number of fee farm rents which had previously been paid to the Crown in the counties of Stafford, Worcester, Leicester, Hereford and Warwick. By 1946, only the payment from Warwick was still being paid as all the others had been lost or redeemed. Someone in Eastbourne claimed to have an oak bureau with a plaque under one of the drawers "*This bureau was made from a piece of the Boscobel oak and given to the Pendrell brothers by King Charles II after the Restoration, 1675."*

Personally, all I can add to the story is that in London in the interesting Church of St Giles in the Fields (situated in St Giles High Street near Charing Cross Road) I recently viewed the tombstone of Richard Pendrell, placed in a porch for safety. On the stone it states Richard Pendrell *"Preserver and Conductor to his majesty King Charles the Second after his escape from Worcester Flight"* died in 1671. Any one who tires of shopping in Oxford Street can easily make a slight detour and visit this interesting church where they can buy a small guide book which devotes a small paragraph to *"the woodman of Boscobel"* whose descendents had such a long association with the Charity of King Henry VIII.

THE LAST TEN YEARS 1985-1995

In my opinion, the history of the Charity since 1985 has been so interesting that I felt a complete chapter should be devoted to it. On several occasions the Charity has been headline news in the local press and many local people know nothing concerning the history of the Charity except that which has happened in the last few years.

The Regulatory Scheme in use in 1985 had been set up in 1978. The details were –

1) 50% of the distributable income should go to the Churches – St Mary's, St Nicholas'and Budbrooke.

2) 30% should be transferred to the Warwick Schools Foundation.

3) 20% should be 'The Town Share' and be spent on items such as repairs of historic buildings, relief of the sick and aged, improved leisure and educational facilities or any other charitable purpose deemed to be for the benefit of the inhabitants.

In the years between 1978 and 1983 the total income of the Charity was still relatively small, that in 1983 being around £27,000. During 1983 land along the Myton Road was sold for housing (the site of Saumur Way etc) and in 1984 the distributable income leapt to over £98,000.

In 1985 when our chapter begins, the figure was around £106,000 in just 3 years the distributable income had quadrupled.

1986 saw various land deals involving much of the land of King Henry VIII Farm along the Myton Road. Following the planning of the M40 motorway, the county council made plans for the diversion of the canal and new link roads to the south, alongside retail development.

To begin with the Charity gave around 6 acres of land to the County Council for roads and traffic islands etc. No compensation was paid because of the likely planning gain arising from the retail park. The Trustees paid the County Council to enlarge sewers etc so that facilities were in place for any future development. This showed condiderable foresight on the part of the Trustees as this expenditure was incurred in advance of any Planning Permissions being obtained.

In 1986 the land was sold for development for 8 million pounds and it is now the site of the Shires Retail Park, incorporating the Sainsbury's store and others nearby. According to Charity Law, money made from such a transaction cannot be distributed, it must be re-invested in other land. The increased income of the Charity came from higher rents and more interest on the additional assets which were purchased as a result of the land sale.

By the following year 1987 the distributable income had doubled to over £878,000. 1988 saw another increase to well over £950,000 and the figure for 1989 topped the million mark for the first time. Since then the figures of the distributable income have exceeded £1,000,000 every year, peaking in 1991 at over a million and quarter when interest rates were high.

With lower interest rates in 1993 the distributable income was still over £1,100,000 and the benefit to the town has continued to be enormous.

The Estate is managed on business lines and if the sale of land or buildings seems advantageous, it will be considered. In 1993 the Charity hoped that plans for development on land it owned adjoining Europa Way, close to the Shires Retail Park, would be included in the current Local District Plan for proposed future development for the years to 2001. When the development was excluded, the Trustees (along with around 200 other businesses, societies and individuals) made a formal objection at the Public Enquiry held in Leamington Town Hall. This was what gave rise to the seemingly critical newspaper headlines of the time.

New Property

During the past 10 years, the Charity has been run like any modern business and expert consultations have been sought. When the Trustees think that it might be advantageous to purchase new property, feasibility studies are carried out and only if these are favourable are purchases then proceeded with.

In the past few years various properties have been bought including –

Town centre shops and multi-storey offices in Bedworth

A multi-storey office block in Banbury now worth £2,000,000

9 modern industrial/warehouse units in St James Road, Northampton, purchased in 1990 at Auction at a cost of £1,680,000.

3 Retail shops in Bridge Street, Nuneaton, purchased in 1992

7 industrial/warehouse units in Acorn Way, Banbury and 12 smaller units both purchased in 1993 at a total price of over £1,000,000.

However there is one recent purchase which I think is more interesting than most others and that is Wedgnock Rifle Range, on the northern outskirts of Warwick.

In the 12th century the Earls of Warwick enclosed a large deer park at Wedgnock for hunting and the park was subsequently owned by a sucession of noblemen, often by gift of the Crown. In 1602 Sir Fulke Greville was granted Wedgnock Park by Queen Elizabeth I and in 1608 his agent estimated that Wedgnock Park then contained 1500 fallow deer and 108 red deer.

From 1545 the Corporation of Warwick had an interest in Wedgnock Park through King Henry VIII's Charity. They were entitled to tithes amounting to 13sh 4d annually from the herbage and to tithes of 2 bucks and 2 does annually as tithes of the deer park. By the late 19th century much of the land was occupied by farms and the park became considerably reduced in size. Around 1900 a group of local dignitories including Alderman Stanton and Alderman Glover (both Trustees of King Henry VIII's Charity) persuaded the War Office to construct a rifle range on the site; the land being purchased from the Earl of Warwick for the purpose. The Army personnel from nearby Budbrooke Barracks, as well as local militia, volunteer forces and the newly formed Warwickshire Rifle Club were allowed to use the range which had 3 butts, one being 1,000 yards from the firing point.

Throughout the 20th century the range was well used, although Budbrooke Barracks closed down in 1960. In the late 1980s the Ministry of Defence decided to sell the land, over 30 bids being received. King Henry VIII's Charity acquired the 90 acres of pasture and woodland in June 1990 for £316,000 because Adventure Sports Limited were willing to enter into a lease at an economic rent. This made the acquisition an attractive investment for the Charity and today Adventure Sports regularly caters for up to 300 visitors per week who enjoy Clay Shooting, Archery, Motor Sports, Command Tasks and Paintball which involves survival games in which participants shoot their opponents with paintballs instead of bullets. The Muzzle Loaders Association of Great Britain use part of the Wedgnock Range on a semi-permanent basis and old weapons from the 17th, 18th and 19th centuries are fired by enthusiasts – which seems fitting in view of the long history of the site.

THE CHURCH SHARE

By the Scheme of 1978, when income was lower, 50% of the disposable income was payable to the parish of Warwick (St Mary with St Nicholas) and St Michael's Budbrooke. Most of the money was paid out towards the stipends of the clergy and the Custos at St Mary's.

However a variation to this Scheme, dated 31st December 1987, still gave the Anglican churches in Warwick a 50% share, but it was split up differently.

The amount of money forming the church share was divided into 7, with 1/7 going to St Michael's Church at Budbrooke. First the stipend of the vicar was to be paid and a yearly sum of £8,700 to the diocese in respect of the vicarage. "*Any other full time clergyman, deaconess or lay worker*" was also to have their stipend paid with an amount paid towards their housing. The remainder of the 1/7 share was to be paid to the Parochial Church Council at Budbrooke "*for furthering the religious and other charitable work of the Church of England in that Parish.*"

As at present there is no curate at Budbrooke, this means that after the vicar's stipend and the amount for the vicarage has been paid, the rest of the share is paid to the P.C.C.

The stipends of the clergy in the Warwick Team Ministry (St Mary's, St Nicholas and Christ Church, Woodloes Park) of St Paul's and of All Saints, Emscote are paid from the remaining 6/7ths and also yearly sums (as at Budbrooke) towards the vicarages.

When these sums have been taken from the income, 70% of the remaining profit is paid to the Parish of Warwick, for the payment of the salary of the custos, the rest being for church repairs, administration and charity work etc.

The remaining 30% is divided equally between St Pauls and All Saints Emscote and it is given to the P.C.C. in each parish, for use in a similar way.

The Parish of Warwick (St Mary's, St Nicholas' and Christ Church, Woodloes Park)

The parish of Warwick, incorporating St Mary's, St Nicholas' and Christ Church, Woodloes Park, is administered as a whole and as at August 1994, the Rev. Gillian Sanderson is acting team rector, Rev. Andrew Gorham is team vicar and Canon David Brindley is to be appointed team rector in September 1994. At present services for Christ Church on the Woodloes Estate are held in a convenient schoolroom, but the Woodloes vicarage is used by several groups for shorter meetings.

In the Parish of Warwick the problems are quite unlike those of other churches in the area because the two town churches are run side by side; St Nicholas' generally hosting the innovative, more modern services and St Mary's being run on more traditional lines. St Mary's Church is visited by thousands of visitors every year and therefore administration is a costly item, taking around 20% of the income of the Parish.

In 1993 work costing over £90,000 was done; a new exit being constructed in the South Transept, the shop area being closed off and new choir stalls and altar rail purchased. The church is famed for its music and there are many expenses in connection with this.

However although the expenses are considerable, in common with the other local parishes, the parish of Warwick regularly sends thousands of pounds to local charities.

At the end of 1992 (in the Parish Magazine) the P.C.C. estimated the principal items of income for the year as £30,000 from church collections and covenanted giving, £3,000 from entry fees to the church tower and £5,000 from the bookstall. The income from King Henry VIII Charity was estimated at £255,000.

On a superficial level some might think that there was no need to give money personally to a wealthy church, but I know from speaking to the C. of E. clergy in Warwick that they all feel that the various congregations ought to give enough money for the running of their own church. If the money from the charity arrives on top of that, it should be used for major maintenance problems, large purchases to benefit the parishioners or given to local charities as appropriate.

It must be remembered that an ancient church which means as much to a town as St Mary's does to Warwick needs a large sum of money each year to enable large and essential items of maintenance to be completed. Also the administration costs are high as there is a full time office manager, a part time secretary and a part time parish administrator. Sometimes special church services need to be arranged, ocasionally in the open air, as in June 1994 when 7,000 people attended a drumhead service commemorating D.Day, which was held in the Market Square,

As in most churches, the vast majority of church workers are volunteers and many, such as the hardworking church guides, give freely of their time every week. Led by Ralph Thornton, a number of men and women are on duty for two hours at a time and perform an invaluable service answering innumerable questions from visitors and also keeping a watchful eye on the church.

Like many other local people, I have many happy memories of St Mary's Church, many of them arising from special schools services I attended, whilst as a pupil and a teacher in Warwick.

AS PART OF THE REFURBISHMENT WORK AT ST MARY'S IN EARLY 1994, THE SHOP WAS PARTITIONED OFF. KAY PRENTICE THE PARISH OFFICE MANAGER IS PICTURED INSIDE SOON AFTER WORK WAS COMPLETED. (Photograph courtesy of Leamington Spa Courier)

THE CUSTOS OF ST MARY'S, JOHN SNELLING, IS PICTURED IN APRIL 1994, STANDING NEAR TO THE ALTAR RAIL AND CHOIR STALLS WHICH WERE INSTALLED AT A COST OF AROUND £50,000. To the right is the pulpit, donated by the Freemasons in 1897, which had been moved to a more prominent position. Some of the wood used in the pulpit was said to be from the Gospel Oak in Chantry Wood, Stoneleigh. (Photograph courtesy of Leamington Spa Courier)

St Nicholas' Church

Following the fire in 1970 which destroyed St Mary's Church Rooms in The Butts and the sale of St Nicholas' Church Rooms in Gerrard Street, some multi-purpose church buildings were needed. This problem was solved in the mid 1970s by the adaptation of St Nicholas' Church into a series of smaller rooms. Toilets were provided and the chancel was blocked off, the nave providing the area for services. In 1988 following the great increase in the amount of money available from King Henry VIII's Charity, two meeting rooms were built and an upper floor constructed over the former chancel. A kitchen was sited upstairs and the old gallery was used for a choir vestry and to house the parish records.

Today the upper room in the former chancel has a wonderful atmosphere, with the stained glass windows being adjacent to the floor area. Although some people do not like the alterations, I must say that I do and the ground floor can be used for parish meetings of all types, besides church services.

AT THE ST NICHOLAS' CHURCH "MOTHERS AND TODDLERS GROUP"
MEETINGS THE CHILDREN PLAY HAPPILY IN A CARPETED ROOM,
CONSTRUCTED ABOVE THE FORMER CHANCEL. In June 1993, Group Leader
Linda Trayneir balanced her 18 months old daughter Rebecca on her knee near Stella
Williams (centre) and son Christopher. Debbie Stephenson and daughter Charlotte admired
the stained glass window whilst Harry was quietly absorbed in his own play. (JF)

Quite by chance I attended the Patronal Festival at St Nicholas' Church on 5th December 1993 and to hear young and old alike laughing at various witticisms in the talks concerning St Nicholas by Rev. Andrew Gorham and Stafford Gage, but later to join in a solemn celebration of Holy Communion was a most pleasurable experience. When the ten smallest members of the Sunday School marched in each dressed as St Nicholas, with a red hat and carrying a black sack, there was great applause. After the service there was a patronal cake, as usual baked by Chris Campbell, and I was most amused to see a small queue of the younger choirboys and choirgirls waiting to see if they would be allowed a second slice!

Personalities Connected with the Parish of Warwick

Rev. Gillian Sanderson became a team vicar in the Warwick Team Ministry in 1986. Born in Cleethorpes and educated at Sheffield City Grammar School and St John's College Durham, from 1965 to 1980 she worked as a hospital administrator. Having been made a deaconess in 1982, she served at All Saints Allesley from 1982-86. Gillian was Diocesan Advisor for Women's Ministry 1984-90 and in 1987 she was ordained deacon. Since 1993 she has been acting team rector in Warwick and at Coventry Cathedral on 23rd April 1994 she was one of the first women in Warwickshire to be ordained a priest.

Appropriately for a person who lists "letter writing" as one of her hobbies, Gillian wrote to me recently concerning the importance of the Charity money.

THE REV. GILLIAN SANDERSON,
PICTURED IN APRIL 1994
OUTSIDE THE VICARAGE ON THE
WOODLOES ESTATE IN WARWICK.
(Photograph courtesy of Leamington Spa
Courier)

"It is always difficult to ensure a balance between maintaining historic buildings adequately and presenting the Gospel message in a challenging and lively way for the 20th century.

Henry's money has, in my view, enabled us as a parish to take seriously our responsibility to maintain beautiful historic buildings as well as enable us to develop a vision for ecumenical activities on the Woodloes Estate. It is a balance which always causes lively debate but one we must maintain, if we are to present the Gospel message to those who need it in today's pressurised society."

The Rev. Andrew Gorham has the distinction of being the only member of the Warwick clergy to live in a vicarage still owned by the Charity of King Henry VIII. The Deanery was sold and a smaller, more modern house was built in part of the garden in 1976. Andrew's wife Anne (nee Crocker, an O.G. of K.H.S.) explained to me that when the house was built, the roof was specially designed so that views of St Mary's were not spoiled.

Andrew was born in Maidstone, Kent and he was educated at the Universities of Bristol and Birmingham. In 1979 he was appointed assistant curate at St Mary's Bromley, Kent and from 1982 he was anglican chaplain at Coventry Polytechnic and an honorary chaplain of Coventry Cathedral. He was appointed to his present post in 1987.

The parish administrator is Leslie Whitaker who came to the Warwick area from Oldham in 1958. With his knowledge of parish affairs extending over several decades, Mr Whitaker has been particularly helpful to me with my research.

Budbrooke

From 1545 St Michael's Church Budbrooke has been administered as part of King Henry VIII Charity. In the leaner times, when the profits of the charity were small, Budbrooke had little money for church repairs, but within the last 10 years, various improvements have been carried out.

In August 1994 I had a very helpful interview with the vicar when I learned a huge amount concerning the difficulties of running a country parish. Rev. Terence Johnson became vicar of Budbrooke in 1981 when various modern amenities were lacking. Although the church and vicarage possessed electricity and water, there was no gas or mains sewage. So when increased income came from the Charity, it enabled a long term plan for modernisation to be devised.

In 1986/7 around £70,000 was spent on the Church tower and the bells, some dating to the 17th century, were re-hung with new fittings. In 1989 an extra plot of land was purchased to improve and enlarge the car park and thousands of pounds were spent on a large cess pit situated under the car park. The installation of gas in 1990 meant that a more efficient type of heating could be provided in the church and the new church Centre costing £200,000 was completed in March 1992. Housing several smaller rooms, toilets and a larger hall for functions, it was formally opened on 4th July 1992 by the Bishop of Coventry and Elsie and Harold Richardson, long standing members of the congregation.

When I visited Elsie and Harold in August 1994, Elsie made me smile as she described the opening of the hall.

> *"Harold cut the ribbon and opened the doors, but they had forgotten how small I was. I could not reach to unveil the plaque without the Vicar's assistance."*

87 year old Elsie had many kind remarks to make about King Henry VIII's Charity. Having lived in Budbrooke since 1938 (36 years in a farm house) and having written two books on the history of the church and village, she gave me much additional information. I felt privileged to visit this amazing octagenarian, who had been up in a glider and a micro-light, as well as attending yoga lessons and completing paintings, besides all her other work for Budbrooke Church, including running the Mother's Union.

As to other expenditure, Rev. Johnson explained that each phase of the building work was planned and it was now the nave and main church building which needed refurbishment. However not all the Henry VIII money was spent in the village and each year thousands of pounds had been given to charities and Christian Missions by the P.C.C. No less than 21 charities benefited from donations from Budbrooke P.C.C. during 1993, the total amount sent being over £14,000.

THE NEW CHURCH CENTRE AT BUDBROOKE WAS OFFICIALLY OPENED ON 4TH JULY 1992 BY THE BISHOP OF COVENTRY AND HAROLD AND ELSIE RICHARDSON, LONG-ESTABLISHED MEMBERS OF THE CONGREGATION. (JF)

St Paul's

St Paul's Parochial Church Council has tried to keep separate the Charity money available to it since 1987 and when I visited the church in August 1994 the vicar Rev. Stephen Hewitt explained to me how a scheme for its administration had been devised.

A former P.C.C. member Miss Kathleen Carter who died in September 1993, an ex-headmistress of Wroxall Abbey School who was said to have been "a woman of vision", had been instrumental in developing this scheme,

The scheme was devised to try to balance the needs of St Paul's and the local community, with claims from the wider locality. Being actively involved in many ventures, Kathleen was able to inform the committee of areas of real need and under her guidance a percentage allocation of funds was developed, which (although not binding) provided a useful check on the way the money from the Charity was spent.

Much as tithes were paid in the past, by the scheme 10% is paid to the Diocese, and a similar percentage is allocated to a Worship Category, which covers such expenditure as hymn books and children's and youth work. 40% is allocated towards maintenance and general improvement of church premises and this has enabled work to be completed on the church hall and it will support the development of a ˙Remembrance Garden in the near future.

ALTHOUGH PART OF THE BUILDING IN FRIAR STREET DATES BACK TO 1824, THE FIRST VICAR OF ST PAUL'S WAS APPOINTED IN 1849. I am particularly interested in St Paul's Church as my grandparents were married there. (JF)

38% is allotted to community needs and each claim is judged on its merits and whether a sufficient link exists with St Paul's. By means of this fund, grants ranging from £100 to £6000 have been given to many voluntary bodies serving Warwick and the wider community including Care, Crossroads, Alcohol Advisory Service, Oken's Charity, St John's Ambulance and the building appeals of some churches in the Deanery. If a sufficient link with the parish can be established 2% is donated to help overseas needs.

This mode of allocating funds has been acclaimed by many people, but not everyone agrees that the money should be used in this way. I wished I had been able to meet the late Kathleen Carter for it seemed that the allocation scheme at St Paul's owed a great deal to her leadership and great moral strength.

All Saint's Church, Emscote

Each of the Church of England Parishes in Warwick has different problems and in Emscote in 1987 a new church building was needed.

ALL SAINTS CHURCH AT EMSCOTE WAS COMPLETED IN 1989 AND THE MODERN DESIGN INCORPORATES MANY ENERGY SAVING DEVICES. The stone altar is placed centrally in the circular sanctuary and above the tabernacle on the rear wall is a striking sculpture, by retired surgeon Dr Charles Kelsey, which portrays the risen Christ with attendant angels. (JF)

The previous church had been demolished in 1968 and for nearly 20 years the congregation had used a converted school building. The parishioners had raised around £100,000 but this was insufficient for a building of any quality.

Since 1987 most of the money from King Henry VIII Charity has been used to service a loan and pay interest charges which were incurred when the fine modern church building was constructed in 1988.

The architect Brian Rush designed a building which was modern in concept as well as design. Materials were chosen with reduced maintenance costs in mind and internal lighting was planned to reduce energy consumption. The exterior is in dark red Redland bricks, with a roof of Redland tiles. A large dome light has a stainless steel spire and cross above.

The main church area inside is square and there is seating in pews for 120 people, with additional seating available if required.

Also incorporated in the church is a Day Chapel, a kitchen, meeting room, parish office, vestries and a committee room. The multipurpose All Saints Church was completed in July 1989 and today it serves the needs of a lively parish community.

As with the other parishes, substantial donations are made by the P.C.C. to local charities. The vicar, Father Lury, now has a curate to assist with duties and once again the increased revenue from the charity has made a huge difference to the prosperity of the church and the parish.

THE SCHOOLS SHARE

Since 1978 the Warwick Schools Foundation, that is Warwick School, The King's High School For Girls and Warwick Preparatory School, has received 30% of the distributable income of the Charity. That has meant that since 1987, varying sums of well over a quarter of a million pounds have been transferred annually to be spent as the Governors of the Warwick Schools Foundation think fit.

Some of this income has been spent on capital building projects and all three schools have had major refurbishments and new buildings within the last few years. Also the two senior schools at present offer Assisted Places under the current Government scheme and in case a future Government ever abolished the Assisted Places Scheme, some money has been put aside into a contingency fund. In future this fund could be used to provide bursaries to assist needy pupils. Currently about 150 pupils at each school are in receipt of bursaries and the great majority of these are Assisted Places via the Government Scheme.

To put the money from King Henry VIII's Charity into perspective, until 7 years ago, Sir Thomas White's Charity paid out more money to the Warwick Schools Foundation. However since 1988 the huge increase in distributable income has meant that around 2 million pounds has been paid to the Foundation by King Henry VIII's Charity and of this around 1 million pounds has been spent on new buildings in the past 5 years.

MUSIC TEACHER PAUL RUSSELL WITH THE WARWICK SCHOOL BIG BAND, FORMED IN MAY 1994. The 17 piece band which plays the music of Benny Goodman and others is led by baritone saxophonist Nigel Raine aged 18, pictured centre. From left to right the other players are (Back row) Tom Greestock, Drew Webber, Paul Davis, Christopher Skilbeck, Colin Johnston, Thomas Christopher, Ross Mason, Edward Holmes, Richard Reynolds. (Front row) Kiran Choudrie, Simon Buczacki, Robert Cobley, David Holdback, Michael Lancaster. William Greestock and Edward Compton were missing from the picture. (Photograph courtesy of Leamington Spa Courier)

Warwick School

Today Warwick School has just over 1,000 pupils, around 200 of these being in the Junior School (ages 7+ to 10+). The attractive 50 acre site now includes a new swimming pool, built in 1991 at a cost of around £828,000, with £300,000 coming from the Warwick Schools Foundation's share of distributable income of King Henry VIII's and other charities. Also a Sports Hall has recently been completed in 1994.

The present headmaster is Dr Philip Cheshire who was appointed in 1987. Having been born in Lincoln and educated at Oakham School, King's College, St Bartholomew's Hospital Medical College and London University, Dr Cheshire is a well known physicist. In 1969 he was a Physics lecturer at St Bartholomew's Hospital Medical College and Senior Research Officer at Huntingdon Research Centre. His published works include various items on cancer research and prior to

DR PHILIP CHESIRE (CENTRE) HEADMASTER OF WARWICK SCHOOL, IS PICTURED FOLLOWING SPEECH DAY OCTOBER 1993. Others in the photograph are (left to right) Adam West, Head Boy; Robert Sheldon, Deputy Head Boy; Viscount Daventry, Lord Lieutenant of Warwickshire, the Speechday guest; and Don Fuller, Chairman of the Foundation Governors. (Photograph courtesy of Leamington Spa Courier)

coming to Warwick, he taught at Rugby School as Physics master from 1972-1980 and Head of Science from 1980 to 1988.

When I first spoke with him in 1993 he gave me a far clearer view of the problems of running a school such as Warwick. He pointed out that Warwick School had an annual turnover from fees in the region of 4 million pounds. Looked at in this context, the share of the King Henry VIII's money did not form a major part of the school's income and was not as important as was sometimes suggested. However there was no doubt that the money eased the situation faced by the Foundation Governors each year and it assisted in supporting with bursaries those in need and in the financing of new buildings.

The King's High School

There are at present around 570 girls in the school, with ages ranging from 11 to 18 and since 1987 when Mrs Jacqueline Anderson took over as headmistress many changes have taken place.

Born in Orpington, Kent, she was educated at Chislehurst and Sidcup Girls

School and Keele University. From 1963-69 Mrs Anderson taught at Bedales School in Hampshire and from 1975-80 she was at Burgess Hill School. Following a spell at the Francis Holland School in London in 1982 she became vice principal of Cheltenham Ladies College in 1983, where she remained until coming to Warwick.

In 1991 when the new Language Block adjoining Chapel Street was built at a cost of about £820,000, around £200,000 was allocated from the Warwick Schools Foundation's share of King Henry VIII's and other Charity funds. The new Red Corridor was completed in 1993 as was the Tomlinson Laboratory named after Dr Muriel Tomlinson (1921-1928) a distinguished Old Girl who died in 1991, after giving 38 years of service as a Governor of the Warwick Schools Foundation.

Since 1990 there have been numerous alterations to some of the older rooms, including the original attics in Landor House, which have been turned into music practice rooms by the use of hardboard and carpets. The main staircase and landing in Landor House has been carpeted and the 300 year old oak banisters stripped of the dark paint. The old Demonstration Room has been dismantled, the Black

MRS JACKIE ANDERSON (RIGHT) HEADMISTRESS OF THE KING'S HIGH SCHOOL, IS PICTURED IN OCTOBER 1993 FOLLOWING SPEECH DAY. Others in the photograph (from the left) are Julia Cleverdon, the Chief Executive of 'Business in the Community' and the Speechday guest; Caroline Dow (Deputy Head Girl); Dawn Brown (Head Girl) and Katie Greenland (Deputy Head Girl). (Photograph courtesy of Leamington Spa Courier)

Country Museum in Dudley using the desk tops and some timbers in St James' Victorian Primary Schools project and the space occupied by Cottage Cloakroom since 1902 is now used as an additional office.

In 1994 the uniform began to be changed from grey and yellow to navy and jade green, but for some years the sixth form, using Red House as their base, have dispensed with uniform altogether.

Another innovation was the use of the Butterworth Hall in Warwick University for Speech Day in 1993 and Mrs Anderson was kind enough to invite me to a most interesting occasion.

THIS PHOTOGRAPH SHOWS TWO TALENTED NETBALL TEAMS FROM KING'S HIGH SCHOOL IN FEBRUARY 1994. The players in dark shirts are the Under 19s and from the left they are Joanna Francis, Deborah Middleton, Katy Shanahan, Melissa Elliott, Samantha Healey, Zoe Bolton (Middle row) Natasha Nolan, Elizabeth Wild, Laura Ballinger and Clare Wilson. The Players in white Shirts are the Under 14s and from left they are Holly Laws, Emily Cooper, Sophie Randolph, Claire Franklin, Madeleine Macdonald, Helen Turner, Emma Saywell and Victoria Smith. The Under 19 team won the West Midlands title and the Under 14s were runners up in their section. (Photograph courtesy of Leamington Spa Courier)

Warwick Preparatory School

In 1981 Miss Elizabeth Major was appointed headmistress and in recent years she too has presided over numerous changes to the school.

With a degree in Education from Bristol University, Miss Major taught Biology at Bedford Modern School (which caters for boys from 7 to 18 years) from 1969 to 1981. She also held the position of head of the Middle School. Some years after her appointment to Warwick, in 1990 Miss Major was appointed Chairman of the Incorporated Association of Preparatory Schools (600 schools worldwide) and was the first woman to become Chairman in the 100 years of its existence.

In 1987 the Administration Block and the Lower School Assembly area was completed and also a Nursery Department for 3 year olds. In 1989 a new nursery building was opened by Miss Smalley and 1990 saw the Science, Art and Technology Block opened by Princess Anne. In 1992 a Sports Hall, which is shared with the King's High School, was completed, this building having been granted £300,000 of the King Henry VIII and other charity money by the Warwick Schools Foundation.

What of the future? Miss Major, now Mrs Prichard after her marriage in 1992, seemed quite clear in her objectives when I spoke to her recently.

ON THURSDAY JULY 5TH 1990 THE PRINCESS ROYAL OPENED THE SCIENCE, AND TECHNOLOGY CENTRE AT WARWICK PREPARATORY SCHOOL. In this photograph (from left to right) are teacher Mrs J. Lillyman, Princess Anne, headmistress Miss Elizabeth Major (now Mrs Prichard) and Peter Barton, Chairman of W.P.S. Governors. The two pupils are Helen Kirby (left) and Natasha Murphy. (Photograph by courtesy of Leamington Spa Courier)

LIKE MANY OTHER MODERN SCHOOLS, WARWICK PREPARATORY SCHOOL INCORPORATES LINKS WITH INDUSTRY IN TECHNOLOGY STUDIES. In the spring of 1994 these 5 girls and other classmates produced baseball caps carrying the school name and squirrel badge at the local embroidery firm of Bryant and Tucker. The girls were involved in every stage of production of the caps and the finished items were sold in the school shop. From left to right the girls are... (Front row) Charlotte Claridge, Amy Robbins and Kate Parton ... (Back row) Claire Roles and Francesca McVeigh. (Photograph courtesy of

"I do not think the school should grow any bigger in the foreseeable future. Our priority is to replace the existing prefabricated rooms with brick buildings" she explained.

The school has around 450 pupils aged between 3 and 11. Boys stay until the age of 7 when they are old enough to transfer to the Junior Department of Warwick School and girls stay until the age of 11 when they take entrance examinations to various secondary schools. Pupils are admitted on a strict rota of admission and although each class has around 22 pupils, these are split into smaller teaching groups, so that pupils can work at their own pace. Specialist subject teaching is available from the age of 7.

The surroundings were modern, yet I was pleased to see a framed tapestry picture of a squirrel on a wall in a prominent place in Mrs Prichard's study. This was the original school badge which had been worked by Miss Smalley many years previously and I felt that a school which remembered its founder in this way had much of which to be proud.

THE TOWN SHARE

Some of the most interesting expenditure of all concerning the Charity of King Henry VIII has occurred in the past 10 years and I have had a hard task in selecting items to include. Requests are considered carefully, the criteria being that the money must be spent to benefit citizens of Warwick, but grants will not be given to projects where public money ought to be used.

In the past few years the total annual amount spent on the Town Share has been in excess of £200,000 and although the vast majority of grants were to organisations, occasionally an individual resident of Warwick was given a grant, perhaps to complete further studies or repair a listed building.

In this chapter I have space only to mention a few of the projects which have received grants in the past 10 years. With the Church of England churches in Warwick included in the main scheme, most of the other churches have had grants at some time or another, as have most of the schools.

Purchase of the Doll Collection in 1987

In 1955 Joy Robinson acquired the lease of Oken's House in Castle Street for her marvellous collection of dolls and toys which she had collected since her childhood. Oken's House very soon became known as "The Doll Museum" and it attracted numerous visitors each year.

TEDDY AND HIS SMALL DOG FIFI ARE EXTREMELY POPULAR WITH VISITORS TO THE DOLL MUSEUM. Teddy has a fawn plush body, button eyes and a stitched mouth, whilst his paws are made from leather. His red flannel overcoat has mother of pearl buttons and underneath Teddy has a cream knitted sweater and trousers whilst green knitted socks complete his outfit. Fifi also is made from plush and both date from the early 20th century. In 1987 King Henry VIII's Charity gave a grant towards the purchase of this and the other items in the collection. (Reproduced by permission of Warwickshire County Museum)

In 1978 Joy Robinson died and although her sister Peggy Nesbitt and her husband kept the museum going for some years, by 1985 she wished to retire and there was talk of the unique collection being sold at auction.

Fortunately Mrs Nesbitt eventually decided that it would be best if her sister's collection was kept intact in its Warwick home and Dr Allan, the County Council Museum Curator, recommended to his committee that an attempt be made to raise the money to purchase the collection. It was a tall order as £55,600 was needed to purchase the collection, with more for the lease of the house and alterations. In the early summer of 1987 there was little County Council cash to spare, but within 4 months the total had been raised, with King Henry VIII's Charity contributing the largest amount ... £16,000. Other large contributions were received from the National Art Collections Fund, The Museums and Galleries Commission, National Heritage Memorial Fund, and various local businesses.

The King Henry VIII All Weather Pitch

In November 1989 the first All Weather Pitch in Warwickshire (5 years later there is still only 1 other) was opened in St Nicholas' Park, Warwick, close to the Sports Hall and Swimming Pool. The fact that the Charity gave a grant of £80,000, matching the £80,000 given by the District Council, with the Sports Council granting £50,000, was recognised by the choice of name.

The Sportturf surface covers an area 106 metres by 64 metres, surrounded by netting and the pitch has floodlighting so it can be used after dark. Either a hockey or football match is able to take place at any one time and several tennis courts are also provided. The pitch is administered from the Main Sports Hall in St Nicholas' Park and the Charity also gave a grant towards the changing rooms. In both the case

THE POPULAR CLIMBING WALL IN THE SPORTS HALL IN ST NICHOLAS PARK WAS OPENED IN APRIL 1993 BY SIR PETER YARRANTON, THEN HEAD OF THE SPORTS COUNCIL. The wall, which has an area of 100 sq metres, was purchased with a grant provided by King Henry VIII's Charity after a request was made by Warwick Climbing Club. Shown in the picture from left to right are Dave Button, Barry Woodbridge and Alistair Latchem. (Photograph courtesy of Leamington Spa Courier)

of the All Weather Pitch and the Climbing Wall in the Sports Hall, the initial request to the Charity came from local clubs – Warwick Hockey Club and Warwick Climbing Club.

By speaking to Peter Cutts of the Amenities Department at Warwick District Council, I had a far better understanding of many of the problems associated with the development of new facilities. He stressed that the role of King Henry VIII's Charity was an enabling one, giving an injection of money which encouraged the remainder of the necessary expenditure to flow from other sources.

IN JULY 1994 A MOST EXCITING MATCH IN M.C.C.L. (DIV TWO) SAW WARWICK CRICKET CLUB DRAW WITH TAMWORTH, THE SCORES BEING LEVEL AT 215. In this photograph the bowler for Warwick is Kevin Clark, with Colin Clark being the wicket keeper. In recent years Warwick Cricket Club has had grants towards wicket covers, sight screens and all weather pitch. The cricket ground at Hampton Road (shown here) was established in 1864 and in 1960 became home to the newly formed Warwick Cricket Club and also Warwick Hockey Club. (Photograph courtesy of Observer Newspaper)

THIS ARCH, ERECTED AROUND 1900, PROCLAIMING 'FRIENDS MEETING HOUSE' LEADS THE WAY TO ONE OF MY FAVOURITE GARDENS AND CAFES. Since 1991 the Quaker Centre in High Street has had several grants towards rebuilding work, furnishing the modern, community cafe and the consequent restoration of the garden, with its old well, clipped yew trees and peaceful atmosphere. There has been a Quaker Community in Warwick since the mid 17th century and the mellow brick Meeting House at the rear dates to 1695. (JF)

The Court Leet

Originally granted to the Earl who was the Lord of the Manor, the Court Leet was anciently presided over by the Earl's Steward, but in 1554, by the Charter of Queen Mary, the Lordship of the Leet was granted to the Corporation. This meant that the Mayor was the High Bailiff and the Town Clerk the Steward, whose job it became to run the Court once a year or more frequently. The Court Leet of Warwick has never ceased to function and it is now one of the few such courts left in the country.

The annual meeting, open to the public, is held in October and there are at present 24 persons on the Jury. The Jury holds the office for life and the court provides an opportunity for townspeople to present items concerning town life which require attention.

As the Court Leet Jury fulfils certain Civic engagements in St Mary's Church, it was felt appropriate that they should have an official badge which would make them instantly recognisable to the general public. A Warwick silversmith designed a badge around 2 1/2 inches in diameter, carrying the bear and ragged staff emblem. Made of solid silver, the cost of the badges has been met by the Jury members themselves and a substantial grant from King Henry VIII's Charity.

IN 1987 ST MARY IMMACULATE R.C. CHURCH IN WEST STREET HAD A GRANT TOWARDS REPAIRS TO THE BELFRY AND CLEANING THE STATIONS OF THE CROSS. Some of these 14 paintings can be seen against the far wall in this recent photograph showing part of the interior of the church. (JF)

THE DISCOVERY OF STRUCTURAL DEFECTS MEANT THAT PARTIAL REBUILDING OF NORTHGATE METHODIST CHURCH TOOK PLACE IN 1992. King Henry VIII's Charity gave a grant towards this vital work and this photograph shows the Civic procession at the re-opening in January 1993. From left to right are Douglas Thornton, Assistant Sergeant at Mace; Derek Fletcher, Sergeant at Mace; Michael Gaffney, Town Clerk; Neil Thurley, Mayor; Graham Sutherland, Beadle; and the Councillors led by J. Savery and Mrs Leddy. (Photograph courtesy of Observer Newspapers)

The County Record Office

Warwick is most fortunate in having a wonderful collection of documents concerning past history of the area and many of these are now in the Warwickshire County Record Office, in purpose built premises opened in 1974, built on the site of the old Priory.

Since that time the staff have had a huge task trying to catalogue and store many interesting documents and collections including the Warwick Castle Archives, acquired in 1978 and the Graham photographic negatives in 1987. In 1991 King Henry VIII Charity helped enormously by giving a grant which helped to provide the services of an additional archivist who catalogued the various documents concerning Warwick Charities. Like other writers and historians I have found the additional lists invaluable and I feel sure in future decades they will be much appreciated.

The Charity has also helped to fund other historical projects including the publication of the booklet "To Divers Good Uses" by Rosemary Booth in 1993 and The Dugdale Society book "The Great Fire Of Warwick 1694" edited by Michael Farr (the ex-County archivist) in 1992.

"THE MEETING POINT"CAFE HAS WONDERFUL VIEWS OF LANDOR HOUSE AND EASTGATE AND I LOVE TO SIT AT THIS PARTICULAR TABLE. Some years ago the Castle Hill Baptist Church purchased the former 'Castle Arms' public house and in 1992 a grant was given by King Henry VIII's Charity to help refurbish the ground floor. Entirely staffed by Christian volunteers, the well appointed Church cafe attracts many local people and visitors. (JF)

FOLLOWING REDEVELOPMENT, THE REGIMENTAL MUSEUM OF THE QUEEN'S OWN HUSSARS IN THE CHAPLAINS' HALL IN THE LORD LEYCESTER HOSPITAL WAS REOPENED IN NOVEMBER 1988 BY THE COLONEL-IN-CHIEF, QUEEN ELIZABETH, THE QUEEN MOTHER. The museum, which was given a grant by King Henry VIII's Charity, has several realistic tableaux including this which depicts part of the Regimental Stables at Hounslow Barracks in 1885, complete with horse dung and various sound effects such as bugle calls and impatient horses. (JF)

Monty's Memorabilia Protected in the Regimental Museum

Having been commissioned into the Royal Warwickshire Regiment in 1908, Field Marshal Viscount Montgomery of Alamein paid many visits to Warwick and the Regiment's Depot at Budbrooke Barracks. Today the Regimental Museum on the upper floor of St John's House houses many souvenirs of the great man whom many believe to have been one of the greatest battlefield commanders this century.

"Monty" as he was affectionately known by millions was a hero for many during the Second World War and it was he who (under the overall leadership of General Eisenhower) commanded the Allied land forces at the D.Day Invasions in Normandy in June 1944 and took the surrender of the German Troops on Luneberg Heath on 4th May 1945. Immensely popular with his troops, the teetotal, anti-smoking vegetarian was a great disciplinarian and after the war he visited Warwick on numerous occasions. In October 1945 he was personally granted the freedom of the Borough of Warwick and in 1955 he presented the prizes at Warwick School.

GENERAL SIR BERNARD MONTGOMERY SPEAKING TO WAR CORRESPONDENTS IN NORMANDY JUST AFTER D. DAY JUNE 1944. This typical photograph of "Monty" is one of several in the Regimental Museum at St John's House. (Photograph by courtesy of the Imperial War Museum, London)

THE PRIME MINISTER, WINSTON CHURCHILL, WALKING WITH GENERAL MONTGOMERY IN NORMANDY JUNE 1944. The copy of this historic photograph in the Warwickshire Regimental Museum in Warwick has a caption underneath which mentions that it was possibly the first time that an officer had been on parade with an umbrella. (Photograph by courtesy of the Imperial War Museum, London)

The Regimental Museum also covers the history of the Royal Warwickshire Regiment from its formation in 1674, through its incorporation into the the Royal Regiment of Fusiliers in 1968 to the present day. There are many other interesting exhibits such as biscuits issued before Dunkirk in 1940 and two caps worn by Brigadier J.P. Duke, D.S.O., M.C., during the First World War. The cap worn by the (uninjured) Brigadier at Zonnebeke Ridge, Ypres in October 1914 had a hole made by a bullet and the cap he wore at Neuve Chapelle in March 1915 had a hole made by shrapnel.

All the important mementoes of Viscount Montgomery and the numerous other exhibits are now protected by superior surveillance equipment and burglar alarms …partly paid for by two grants from the Charity of King Henry VIII.

IN 1993 THE CHARITY GAVE A GRANT TOWARDS THE PUBLICATION OF A GUIDE BOOK FOR THE REGIMENTAL MUSEUM OF THE QUEEN'S OWN HUSSARS. Primarily aimed at young people, the guide book is being discussed in this photograph (from left) by Don Fuller, Chairman of King Henry VIII Charity Trustees; Col. Hugh Sanders, Managing Trustee of the Queen's Own Hussars Collection; Councillor Agnes Leddy, Mayor of Warwick and her Husband Ted. On the right is Paul Barker, consultant to the Queen's Own Hussars and a former Curator of Warwick Castle. (Photograph courtesy of Leamington Spa Courier)

GARDEN HISTORIAN SUSAN RHODES AND VOLUNTEER GARDENER GEOFF CROWE EXAMINE THE REMAINS OF A HYPOCAUST IN THE LORD LEYCESTER HOSPITAL GARDEN. Once used to help cultivate pineapples, the heated trench is now a great rarity. The Charity gave a grant to help restore the ancient and interesting garden which is proving to be a great tourist attraction. (Photograph courtesy of Leamington Spa Courier)

The Lord Leycester Hospital Garden

It is always exciting when an enthusiast is determined to establish an entirely new venture and so it was in 1994 when Susan Rhodes, a garden historian and the wife of the Master of the Lord Leycester Hospital, attempted to restore a centuries-old garden adjoining the medieval buildings. An ancient dovecot, mentioned in deeds connected with King Henry VIII's Charity in 1565, and subsequently adapted into a Victorian gazebo had been restored in 1989 with the aid of a charity grant. In early 1994 Mrs Rhodes organised restoration and the re-planting of the garden with the aid of a further grant from King Henry VIII's Charity, the Chairman of the Trustees Mr Don Fuller planting one of the magnolia trees. The garden, still in the course of restoration, first opened to the public on 2nd April 1994, a cold, wet and windy Easter Saturday. I was proud to be amongst the very first visitors to this exciting project and I feel sure that in future this acre of unusual garden will be one of the major tourist attractions of the town.

THIS DELIGHTFUL SCENE AT THE SALTISFORD CANAL TRUST ILLUSTRATES HOW HARD WORK AND IMAGINATION CAN TRANSFORM AN AREA. I am assured that Sid the resident goose (so called because he is vicious) is around 30 years old. (Photographed by Bryan Hicks, Leamington Spa)

The Saltisford Canal Trust

In February 1982 the "Coventry Evening Telegraph" ran a small article headed "Jobless man plans canal venture". The man was Dick Amende and today he is the full time manager of the Saltisford Canal Trading Company which manages the Saltisford Arm of the Grand Union Canal for the Saltisford Canal Trust (a registered charity). Assisted by many willing volunteers and other charities, Dick Amende's dream of restoring part of the Warwick terminus of the Warwick and Birmingham Canal eventually became a reality in 1985, after 3 years of hard work, and the flourishing centre which exists today is a tribute to his determination and vision and that of others. Situated close to the junction of the Budbrooke and Birmingham Road, the Saltisford Arm today offers moorings, fishing, a barbecue area and a conservation walk as well as a most interesting information centre and canal museum.

CO-OPERATION AT LANDOR HOUSE ON SEPTEMBER 1ST 1992. On the 300th anniversary of the signing of the agreement to build Landor House, my first book "She Dyed About Midnight" concerning Landor House and the site of King's High School was published. Christopher Jeens (the County Archivist) is shown left, holding the actual document, suitably protected; John Francis (Chairman of K.H.S. Governors) and myself make up the group. King Henry VIII's Charity gave a grant towards the publication and Headmistress Jackie Anderson hosted a reception. (Photograph courtesy of Observer Newspapers)

THE FUTURE

Although I have tried to give a clear outline of the history of this Charity, the subject is so complex, that much had to be omitted for lack of space. Perhaps some will feel that I have over simplified some matters and have left out other important items. However I would like to stress that this book gives a personal view and I will quite understand if general readers, historians and even Trustees of the Charity feel inclined to disagree with me over certain points.

For the 450 years of its existence the Charity has provided the town of Warwick with money and in recent years, the increased income has made an enormous difference to the town. St Mary's and the other Warwick churches in the main have sufficient for the upkeep of their buildings and can give money to other local charities. Warwick School, the King's High School For Girls and Warwick Preparatory School have additional money for buildings and bursaries and the town share of the income has been used for a large variety of worthwhile projects.

Not that the Charity escapes criticism. There are those who say that the Anglican churches, in particular St Mary's and St Nicholas' receive too large a share and some feel that it is wrong to use Charity money to support the Independent Schools of the Warwick Schools Foundation, especially when less than 20% of pupils actually come from Warwick itelf. In 1986/7 the Charity was blamed for encouraging stores to open on "Green Belt Sites", bringing about a fear of degeneration in Warwick and Leamington Town Centres.

However it has become clear to me that if the Trustees of King Henry VIII's Charity had not sold agricultural land for development, some other landowner would have … thus depriving the town of the great financial rewards it has reaped since the land sales. Whether you are in favour of Independent Schools or not, undeniably all three schools in the Warwick Schools Foundation help to bring prosperity to Warwick and keep the name of the town to the fore in educational circles.

Many critics do not understand the ways in which the Charity operates. The Trustees have a legal obligation to administer the assets properly and they need very good reasons to do other than maximise the opportunities to gain best financial advantage for the benefit of the Charity's purposes. The Trustees are obliged to act in accordance with the provisions of the Scheme governing their Charity and if the current Scheme directs that the distributable income is divided in a certain way, then the Trustees are obliged to comply.

The Future Seems Optimistic

One of the most recent grants to be made in 1994 has been to the Warwick Town Partnership, an exciting venture which promises much.

Formed in July 1994, the partners are Warwickshire County Council, Warwick District Council, Warwick Town Council, Warwick Castle and Warwick Chamber of Trade and Commerce. The Partnership is a completely independent agency committed to securing the economic and environmental regeneration of the town and its aim is to make Warwick a centre of excellence for tourists and residents alike. Since the sale of the Castle to the Madame Tussaud's Group in 1978 more visitors than ever have come to a more lively Castle, offering more modern facilities. Warwick has recently been identified as one of 25 towns in England likely to see a great increase in prosperity in future decades.

A Productive Meeting

At 7.30 p.m. on 13th September 1994 around 100 people gathered in the historic Lord Leycester Hospital, for a public meeting to discuss ideas of how to improve the town of Warwick via the newly formed Town Partnership. Copies of the first issue of "Partnership News" were handed out and in that leaflet Jim Skinner, the Chairman of the Partnership, had written,

"We have been most fortunate in securing a grant from King Henry VIII Charity and this, together with contributions from the partners, has enabled us to appoint a Partnership Officer (Alan West) and a Partnership Assistant (Anna Butterworth). Anna will initially have special responsibility for co-ordinating the town's 450th Anniversary Celebrations in 1995."

I thoroughly enjoyed the meeting ... it was the first time I had ever been in the Lord Leycester Hospital at night and the old oak timbers, stone walls and soft lighting created a wonderful atmosphere. Ralph Armond, the General Manager of Warwick Castle, answered several informal queries in a positive and helpful way; Ian Palmer of the local C.W.R. radio station taped much of the proceedings ready for a discussion about Warwick on The Breakfast Show next day and numerous local people such as 85 year old Tom Cox from Pickard Street, who read a carefully worded speech asking for more basic amenities such as food shops, made many valid criticisms.

Apart from the official speakers such as Bryn Brewster, the Mayor of Warwick, there were many local officials in the audience including John Picking, Chief Executive of Warwick District Council and Dr Christine Hodgetts, the Deputy Mayor of Warwick. In all likelihood Dr Hodgetts will be created Mayor of Warwick on the 15th May 1995 – exactly 450 years to the day after Thomas Oken became Chief Burgess and the Charity of King Henry VIII was set up. As a historian and lecturer, locally born Dr Hodgetts will be carrying on the 20th century tradition of having a historian as Mayor in important years in the town's history, such as when

IN JULY 1994 THE WARWICK TOWN PARTNERSHIP WAS FORMED AND THE CHARITY GAVE A GRANT. Representatives from many organisations in the town joined together to promote new ideas, especially for tourism and improved retail opportunities. In this photograph (from the left) are Andrea Mezzone, Warwick Chamber of Trade and Commerce; Derek Forwood, County Council Chairman; Peter Byrd, District Council Chairman; Deborah Germaine, Acting Marketing Manager of Warwick Castle; and Bryn Brewster (seated) the Mayor of Warwick. (Photograph courtesy of Leamington Spa Courier)

Thomas Kemp was Mayor in the Pageant Year of 1906 and George Tibbits officiated in the Coronation Year of 1953.

Just as George Tibbits contacted the citizens of Warwick, Rhode Island U.S.A. and several other towns abroad sharing the name, so representatives of these towns have been invited to attend the celebrations on 15th May 1995. I do hope some are able to come, for it would add an international flavour to celebrations whilst also making another link with the past.

If I have learned anything during my lifetime it is – never underestimate the power of an individual, for some people through their sheer determination achieve an enormous effect on their environment and the lives of others around them. This history of King Henry VIII's Charity contains the story of numerous such committed individuals such as Thomas Oken, John Fisher, Herbert Hill, Thomas Kemp, Eleanor Doorly, George Tibbits, Kathleen Carter and many more, but it is not only the great and good who have affected the lives of others, some seemingly ordinary and uneducated individuals too have had a lasting effect on the town.

The Future Role of the Charity in Warwick

Although it must be stressed that King Henry VIII's Charity is not directly linked to the Town Council in any way, there are many indirect links and I believe the income generated by the Charity will be vital in the future development of the town, just as it was in the past centuries.

Today King Henry VIII's Charity has assets of around 17 million pounds, mostly invested in property, but with several millions in bank accounts for easy access for repairs and expenses. Properly managed, there is every justification for supposing that the Charity will continue to thrive and be able to support new ventures perhaps generated as a result of the Town Partnership. Although a percentage of the current distributable profits of well over 1 million pounds annually is taken up by the stipends of the clergy and other necessary expenditure, there is still a considerable sum left for the churches, schools and town to use. Many towns would love to have such a charity and in future decades I believe the income will be put to good use.

As a final paragraph I will not use vague sentences but will allow the charitable works to speak for themselves. During 1993 the following groups were amongst those helped by grants (Town Share) from the Charity of King Henry VIII ... Warwick Horticultural & Allotments Society, Warwick Tennis Club, Aylesford School, British Red Cross, Central Ajax Football Club, 7th Woodloes Scout Group, Mid Warwickshire Boys Football League, St Mary Immaculate Playgroup, Park View H.E.P., Woodloes First School, Westgate County First School, Warwick Boat Club, Golden Jubilee Club, Warwick O.A.P. Assoc., Coten End First School, James Court Residential Home, Warwick Arts Society, Emscote Rangers F.C., Warwickshire Constabulary Old Folks Christmas Party, West Street Traders Christmas Lights, Coten End Middle School, Amateur Boxing Club, Royal Warwickshire Regiment Old Comrades 1944 Holiday Fund, Aylesford Basket Ball Club, All Saints Duke of Edinburgh Club, Warwick Corps of Drums, Warwick Park

Senior Citizens Assoc., Warwick Relief in Need Charity, Newburgh Middle School and the British Legion. There were numerous other grants from the Town Share including several to the Town Council for Warwick In Bloom, Planting of Road Verges and other items.

Thomas Oken who began the whole thing 450 years ago would have been very proud.

APPROPRIATELY THE CURRENT TRUSTEES AND CLERK & RECEIVER ARE PICTURED IN FRONT OF A PORTRAIT OF THE FOUNDER OF THE CHARITY. From left to right, those standing are Mr N. F. J. Thurley; Mr H. R. C. Walden C.B.E.; Mr T. K. Meredith; Mr B. Brewster and Mr J. P. McCarthy. Those sitting are Mrs M. B. Haywood; Mr B. Gillitt (Deputy Chairman); Mr D. Fuller (Chairman); Mr P. G. Butler (Clerk & Receiver); and Mrs S. M. Rhodes. (Photograph by Simon Photography, Warwick).

ACKNOWLEDGEMENTS

A large number of people have been extremely helpful to me in the compilation of this book especially Donald Fuller, the Chairman of Trustees of King Henry VIII's Charity, and the other Trustees.

The wide local knowledge of Peter Butler, the Clerk to the Trustees of King Henry VIII's Charity, has been invaluable, as has his helpful advice and general enthusiasm. Michael Gaffney, the Town Clerk of Warwick, has given much support both with advice and access to historical items in the Court House. Joan Greenwood has spent a great amount of time in reading the text and I am very grateful to her for undertaking that tedious task. Ralph Thornton has been particularly helpful concerning the history of Warwick School and St Mary's Church, not least by the provision of photographic material.

Much of my research was completed in the Warwickshire County Record Office and I would like to thank Christopher Jeens, the County Archivist, and all the staff, especially Jerry Weber the senior conservator and Timothy Warrender, assistant conservator, who took many of the photogaphs appearing in this book.

Also I would like to acknowledge the help given by many other people including Dr W. Allan (Curator of Warwickshire County Museum), Mrs J. Anderson (Headmistress of King's High School), Mr R. Armond (General Manager) and other staff of Warwick Castle, Dr P. Cheshire (Headmaster of Warwick School), Rev. A. Gorham (Team Vicar of the Parish of Warwick), Rev. S. Hewitt (Vicar of St Paul's, Warwick), Mr T. Horn (Clerk to the Trustees of Oken's Charity), Rev. T. Johnson (Vicar of St Michael's Budbrooke) Father Lury (Vicar of All Saint's, Warwick), Mr A. Measures, Mrs C. E. Prichard (Headmistress of Warwick Preparatory School), Capt. D. Rhodes (Master of the Lord Leycester Hospital), Rev. G. Sanderson (Team Vicar of Parish of Warwick), Miss E. Tibbits, Mr L. Whitaker (Parish of Warwick, Administrator), Head of Local Plans and Tourism (Wyre Forest District Council) and Mr B. Young who loaned me his considerable collection of items concerning Warwick School.

Key to the Source of Photographs from Private Collections

NA – Nancy Allibon, JG – Joan Greenwood, RHT – Ralph Thornton, HW – Herbert Walden, CW – Charles Wiseman, BY – Barry Young. Those labelled JF were taken recently by the author.

BIBLIOGRAPHY

King Henry VIII's Charity (unpublished typescript) – E.G. Tibbits
The Union Catalogue of Warwick Charity Records (unpublished) WCRO
Victoria County History of Warwickshire – Volume 8 and others
The Black Book of Warwick – Ed Thomas Kemp 1898
The Book of John Fisher – Ed Thomas Kemp
History of Warwick and its People – Thomas Kemp 1905
Warwick Charities 1826 – H.M. Commissioners
The Town Maps of Warwick 1610-1851 WCRO
The Town and Castle of Warwick – William Field 1815
Warwickshire (The Buildings of England) – Pevsner & Wedgwood 1966
Around Warwick in Old Photographs – Rosemary Booth 1990
The Great Fire of Warwick (Dugdale Society) Ed. Michael Farr 1992
The Lady Who Fought the Vikings – Don Stansbury 1993
The History of Warwick School – A. Leach 1906
The Book of the Jubilee (K.H.S.) 1929
The King's High School 1879-1979 (The Governors)
History of Budbrooke 1122-1968 – E. Richardson 1968
Budbrooke Past and Present – E. Richardson 1993
The English Way of Death – Julian Litten 1991
A Who's Who of Warwickshire County Cricket Club – Brooke & Goodyear
Great Britons (20th Century Lives) – Oxbury 1985
King Charles II – Arthur Bryant 1931
The Woodcarvers of Warwick – Stevens (Warwick Museum)
Wells and Springs of Warwickshire H.M.S.O. 1928
A Life of Richard Beauchamp – D. Styles, Friends of the Collegiate Church of St
    Mary, Warwick
The Parish Chest – W.E.Tate
Chronicle of the World – Longmans 1989
Chronicle of the Twentieth Century – Longmans 1988
Coventry Evening Telegraph Year Books
Various copies of the Warwick Advertiser & Leamington Spa Courier
Booklets by the Chaddesley Corbett Local History Society
Various directories of Warwickshire & Church Guide Books

INDEX

THIS ATTRACTIVE DRAWING OF THE WARWICK CORPORATION
SEAL APPEARS ON THE MAP OF CHADDESLEY CORBETT DRAWN
BY JAMES FISH IN 1697. The walled town can be clearly seen, as can the
watchman blowing their horns. (Reproduced by permission of Warwickshire
County Record Office)

BY THE SAME AUTHOR

A Tour of St Margaret's Church, Whitnash
Published 1992 (Obtainable from the Church)

She Dyed About Midnight (Warwick)
Published by Brewin Books 1992

Beneath the Great Elms (Whitnash)
Published by Brewin Books 1993